What Would *Love* Do Right Now?

A Guide to Living an Extraordinary Life

Victoria Benoit

Extraordinary Outcomes Publishing, LLC
Phoenix, Arizona

ExtraordinaryOutcomesPublishing.com

What Would *Love* Do Right Now?™

Extraordinary Outcomes
PUBLISHING, LLC

www.ExtraordinaryOutcomesPublishing.com, Phoenix, Arizona

Contributors:
Editor: Paula Hofmeister
Portrait Photograph: Glenn Mire
Cover Design & Book Layout: Betsy McGrew

Printed in the United States of America

Library of Congress Cataloging-in-Publication Data

Paperback ISBN 978-0-9838567-0-2
eBook ISBN 978-0-9838567-1-9
Library of Congress Control Number: 2021903722

Inquiry to Resolution™ and What Would Love Do Right Now?™
are trademarks of Victoria Benoit

This book is dedicated to:
you, the reader, for your courage to
live an extraordinary life;

Sara Godfrey, my mother, for your love and encouragement;

Edward Benoit, Jr., my father, who taught me to
live life as an adventure!

Contents

Preface

Extraordinary lives are filled with adventure. Most adventures have a beginning, middle and an end; however, the adventure in this book has no end. Asking the question *what would love do right now?* is useful at any time, any place, with anyone, from now on. It is so easy to remember, because it is so simple. The key is to remember to use it. Once you get started, it will become so natural that you will find yourself telling those around you about it, or they will say some form of, *"You're so much calmer these days. What are you doing differently?"* This is your opportunity to share how your life has improved by asking this simple question.

The primary benefit of asking yourself *what would love do right now?* is to create your life from the power of love, the real gold of life that makes everything worthwhile.

This book is not for everyone. It is a workbook that requires your active participation. You need to be willing to authentically look within yourself and make changes. Doing a process I call **Inquiry to Resolution**™ requires this willingness. During the inquiry, you may come face to face with old hurts, betrayals, humiliations, disappointments, and confusion—even abuse—that you haven't thought of for a long time or perhaps have buried deep within. Now is the time to release these experiences to free yourself and be all that you can be. The resolution comes by moving down into your heart where compassion and letting go are available through forgiveness and making amends.

During the twenty plus years I have spent coaching and counseling clients, I have found there is no hope in avoidance. Going into the unknown parts of yourself from your past may not be easy; however, it is necessary if you want to live an extraordinary life.

May you have a sense of adventure and wonder as you are reading this book, doing the inquiries, and implementing the question *what would love do right now?* into your daily life. May your inquiry into love have a positive impact on those you love and care about.

Thank you for the opportunity and privilege to make a difference in your life and in the lives of those who are blessed to have you in their lives.

Love and blessings,
Victoria Benoit

Introduction

Living from Your Heart is Possible!

This book is about experiencing love and the gift of the present moment. To have a heart-centered life, the first step is to release all the pain and suffering that still lives in your heart, such as childhood experiences from school and family, as well as hurts from friendships, bosses, employees, clergy, and your romantic relationships.

These experiences are not happening now, and they are not who you are in your essence where you are pure and precious. What good are they doing you today? The past no longer exists…or does it?

You may think that the experiences from the past do not affect your life today, but they affect the very air you breathe. Not only do they affect your present experience of life, they affect your future. How can you have a bright new future if unresolved parts of your past remain? There is no space to create anything new. This makes it difficult to create and develop new plans and goals, and could be why your intentions may not always manifest.

This book is an inner journey into your Self and your life. Some chapters may take more courage than others. You will uncover hurts from your past— some of which may now seem minor all the way to experiences of serious abuse. If at any time you are overwhelmed, I recommend seeking support or professional assistance. The more you allow yourself to explore areas you've been avoiding, the greater the outcome. It is important that you take your time so you can integrate the positive changes you're making.

How I Came to Write this Book

I had been receiving gentle nudges of encouragement from within for a few years to write about living from love—a place that opens up what is possible when one consciously brings love into any situation. Although I had been successfully writing professional articles for six years, the thought of writing from my personal experience was overwhelming. I decided to take Dr. Margaret Mears' 8-week, intensive, creative writing course, *Write from Your Heart*™—not only once, but twice.

I remember welling up with tears the first time I shared with the group what I had written. I felt what I was sharing was so private. I was revealing previously hidden aspects of my creative self. I was coming out as a writer, being seen and known—experiencing a rite of passage.

Later that same year, a book title popped into my consciousness, loud and clear: What Would Love Do Right Now? I grabbed a notebook. I wrote the title and my name on the first page, and then I drew a big heart in the middle of the page. That was in December 2009.

I could not seem to write anything else for months. Then it dawned on me that before I could write about it, I needed to ask myself the question *what would love do right now?*

Boy, did opportunities come to ask myself the question, especially at times when I was so angry I wanted to explode, and times when I felt defeated and wanted to throw in the towel. Each opportunity provided me with validation on the significance, simplicity, and results of asking this question. I then started using this question as an inquiry into all other aspects of my life. It has since become my guide to living an extraordinary life.

In 2010, my friend and colleague, Tarra of Sedona, suggested I attend Tom Bird's retreat, *Write Your Book in 5 Days*™. Although the whole idea of writing my book in five days intrigued me, I was not yet ready.

One year later, the nudge to actually write the book became so strong that I could no longer ignore it. I even had two clients who were on their way to the retreat to write their own books. I found my original notebook, and four months later I was in the retreat myself. This book represents the outpouring of my commitment for everyone to live an extraordinary life.

Note to Reader

How to Use This Book

This step-by-step guide supports releasing and healing your past hurts through a process called Inquiry to Resolution. By moving slowly from your head to your heart and into a place of love, you will discover that life can be an extraordinary adventure. From this heart-centered place, what's available is the gift of the present moment—a place from which to make decisions and establish goals for your life. Then you can use your brain to implement and fulfill your plans.

I am committed to the success of everyone who chooses to do this work. I recognize that each of us have unique life experiences and we interpret relationships with our parents, family, friends, and associates in different ways. For example, parents come in many forms including; biological, step, foster, single, adoptive, same-sex, and guardians. However you define these relationships, your experiences are valid.

In **Chapters 1** and **2,** we define what love is, and discuss forgiveness and making amends. **Chapters** 3-7 explore how you can heal the past through the Inquiry to Resolution process. These five chapters will examine the many relationships in your life, including those associated with your family, romance, career, health, and finances, as well as looking at your responsibility in those relationships. Then **Chapter 8** highlights your self-expression through the experience of creativity, communication, and spirituality. **Chapter 9** focuses on restoring your power in your everyday interactions through recognizing your triggers. The opportunity to design your life is presented in **Chapter 10**. The worksheets for this chapter consist of simple questions with plenty of room for you to free flow your ideas, discoveries, declarations, and any actions you're inspired to take. Starting with your life purpose, you can design your ideal day, home life, career/job, and relationships. Finally, in **Chapter 11** you will create three personal manuals for living your extraordinary life.

I recommend starting at the beginning and going through each chapter at your own pace. Balance is the key! As you are re-evaluating and making changes in your life, it is easy to become overwhelmed and frustrated. Be gentle with yourself, love yourself, and pace yourself. Take your time. This isn't a race. It's a journey into your inner world, where the limitations that stop you from living an extraordinary life are patiently waiting to be transformed. Let the question, *what would love do right now?* become a mantra that you use daily or even hourly, to keep you in your heart.

Inquiry to Resolution Process

To gain the greatest benefit from this book, it's important that you understand the Inquiry to Resolution process. The primary purpose of this process is to identify and resolve those areas of your life where you feel stuck and love is missing. As you examine each area and love becomes more present, your life will begin to flow the way it was intended. It is important that you love and accept all of what is coming up for you—the good, the bad, and the ugly. When releasing your unresolved issues from a place of love, an expansion occurs in your heart and body, whereby love naturally flows through you.

The inquiries in this book are designed as an in-depth approach to releasing past events holding you back from experiencing more love, joy, and freedom today, and creating new actions and projects to express these new possibilities in the future.

The interactive **Inquiry to Resolution** worksheets, that accompany this book, are available at, www.ExtraordinaryOutcomesPublishing.com/forms. Each worksheet begins with an overview of the area you will be exploring and is organized into three sections: Inquiry, Resolution, and Action.

- **Inquiry** is designed to provide insight into what happened at a particular time (past). Making a note of the age at which the incident occurred can help you see it through the eyes of the person you were at that time. You will identify who was there, what actions each person took, and what was said; how you felt; what response(s) you withheld; and what conclusions you came to when that happened.

As emotions surface, ask yourself, *"What am I really feeling?"* For example, if anger surfaces, consider it may be the secondary emotion you feel, because you've not identified and released the underlying feeling(s), such as betrayal, hurt, rejection, humiliation, or abandonment.

- **Resolution** focuses on healing how that incident affects you now (present). It starts with examining how the conclusions you drew at the time of the incident—and the feelings you're still holding onto— are impacting your life today; what you needed emotionally, mentally, physically, or spiritually at that time; and then—in an ideal world— you get to declare what could have been said, or done, that would have made a positive difference for you.

    This is followed by a clearing technique, which invites you to open your heart to love, compassion, and forgiveness for yourself; then provides the opportunity to release the effects of the past and heal your heart.

    The resolution concludes with acknowledging how you feel now.

- **Action** gives you the opportunity to create a plan for moving forward by asking yourself, *"What would love do right now?"* and determining the activities that support you in living an extraordinary life (future). Ideas are just ideas unless you have a plan to implement them.

To get the most out of each Inquiry to Resolution experience, I recommend setting enough time aside to allow yourself to go deep into your inner knowing where all your answers are. Give yourself permission to access the unconscious part of you that knows. You can say to yourself, *"I am ready to know what my life-depleting beliefs are right now."* Then listen, feel, or imagine what they are.

Find a private place where you won't be interrupted. Get comfortable. Close your eyes. Center yourself in the present moment by taking a few deep breaths—

slowly in and out through your nose. This will activate your parasympathetic nervous system, which regulates your body's involuntary muscle reactions, and slows many high-energy functions. In other words, you will be calmer and more relaxed.

The degree to which you participate in each Inquiry to Resolution process is the degree to which you will free yourself from the past. You will then have more room in the present to experience love, optimism, hope, peace of mind, and to create an extraordinary future filled with new possibilities beyond what you ever imagined.

Chart Your Accomplishments and Celebrate

I recommend that you celebrate as a way of congratulating yourself for a job well done when you complete each Inquiry to Resolution. Children love rewards and, I assure you, so does the child within you.

Track your progress by recording how you celebrated and placing a "gold star" on the *What Would Love Do Right Now Accomplishment Chart,* which is available at www.ExtraordinaryOutcomesPublishing.com/forms.

Display the chart where you can see it as a daily reminder of your commitment to living a heart-centered life. Continue the process of giving yourself the acknowledgment and encouragement you deserve until your chart is complete.

My Accomplishment Chart, on the next page, is an example of how I celebrated the healing I experienced upon completing each Inquiry to Resolution provided in this book.

W H A T   W O U L D   L O V E   D O   R I G H T   N O W
Accomplishment Chart

✓	Worksheet	How I Celebrated
★	My Relationship with My Parents	*took day-trip to Sedona with my mom*
★	My Relationships with Others	*went dancing with a group of friends*
★	My Parents' Relationship	*went to the park, fed the ducks, and read a book*
★	My Romantic Relationships	*went for a weekend getaway with my sweetie*
★	My Profession/Work Relationships	*bought myself a new dress*
★	My Health Nutrition	*went for a facial at the spa*
★	My Finances	*went to a movie with my best friend*
★	My Self-Expression Creativity Communication Spirituality	*went to a paint and sip party with a friend* *bought myself a bouquet of flowers* *took a lavender oil bubble bath*
★	Restoring My Power	*went kayaking at the lake with my sweetie*
★	Designing My Life My Purpose My Ideal Day My Ideal Home Life My Ideal Profession/Work My Ideal Relationships	*had mani/pedi at the spa* *went to the theatre with my friends* *went country dancing* *went for a massage* *went up to the cabin with my sweetie*
★	My Extraordinary Life Guide to Daily Living Guide to Romantic, Intimate Relationship Guide to Sexual Satisfaction	*went to my favorite restaurant with a friend* *went to sound healing meditation with a friend* *engaged in a tantric workshop with my sweetie*

1

What is Love?

There are many types of love: love of self, love of your work, love of your parents who gave you life, love of your friends, love of your children, and love of your pets. Then there is romantic love, love of country, and love of God. Each has a different meaning and unique experience. Throughout history, many have attempted to define love. There are biological theories, cultural theories, and psychological theories about various types and styles of love. You name it and someone has written about it. Throughout this book, the word *love* will be used in the process of transforming many areas of your life.

The love I'm speaking about is a heart-centered love—the primal essence of love that permeates all life. It is moving from your head to your heart, surrendering your ego and moving into compassion, understanding, and a deep sense of caring. Asking yourself, *"What would love do right now?"* from this place, allows you to be more loving in all your interactions.

When two lovers are making love, looking into one another's eyes and relishing the moment of bliss, they are sharing their experience together so completely that for them nothing else is happening in the entire world. They are engaging in the primal essence of love, shutting out the outer world—nothing intrudes. They are being present in the moment.

I hope you've had this experience. If not, maybe you've experienced the pure essence of love with a puppy or a newborn baby. This is unconditional love at its finest.

Now that you know the type of love I'm talking about, are you ready to experience it again, or for the very first time? It's really a choice.

You Are Love

Knowing that **you ARE love** can change the course of your life forever. You can never separate yourself from love—ever! Nevertheless, it may seem as though you're separate. It is time to awaken to the love you are—to universal love, the primal essence of love that permeates all life.

Sometimes we feel like love is missing and we look to others to provide it. Actually, look no further, you have everything you need—you are love.

What would life be like if you were to wake up and love governed all of your actions and decisions? What would you do, as love? You might start your day by looking in the mirror and saying, *"I love you."* Perhaps you would meditate or journal in a sacred space. As love, you could jog, walk, or tend your garden in the morning sunlight. You might take some time to go to breakfast with friends or pick up chocolate-covered donuts on the way to work. When you bring the love you are to all areas of your life throughout your day, love is what you will experience moment by moment.

The Power of Love

"Getting gotten" and "being present" are essential to experiencing the power of love. These concepts are defined here for clarity.

The experience of getting gotten occurs when another is so present with you that you feel heard, seen, known, and understood for who you truly are, and know that anything you say or do is accepted as an act of love.

Being present involves a conscious act of awareness—mindfulness. It replaces automatic perceptions of situations with an actual experience of living in the moment. Mindfulness is the art of living right in the center, between past and future—it is living in the present.

Therefore, being present means being fully conscious of who you are, where you are, what you are doing, and whom you are with at that exact moment. No images of the past and no dreams of the future interrupt this awareness. There are no distractions or other places you'd rather be. Nothing else matters. Your body, mind, and heart are one.

The following excerpt from Buddhist literature is offered to illustrate being fully present—what the Buddhists call mindfulness:

> *A man once asked the Buddha, "What are the teachings of you*
> *and your disciples?"*
> *Buddha answered, "We sit, we walk, and we eat."*
> *The man replied, "But, everyone sits, walks, and eats."*
> *The Buddha answered, "Yes, but when we sit, we **know** that we*
> *are sitting. When we walk, we **know** that we are walking.*
> *When we eat, we **know** that we are eating."*

There is nothing like the experience of being present, or the experience of getting gotten! It is the primal essence of love that permeates all life. It is so powerful it takes your breath away.

Love is—the Only Answer

Love is the answer, always and in all ways. Love is all there is, there is nothing else. Love is everywhere and all around us—self-love, love of others, and love of life. You breathe it, see it, smell it, and taste it. Seeing lovers kissing on a bridge; a mother holding her newborn; a teenager helping an older person across the street; a father teaching his child how to ride a bike. It's about creating and experiencing life to the fullest in all its perfection and disappointments.

May this book motivate you to look at your life and evaluate where you are in relation to love and living from the essence of love. I believe that asking the question *what would love do right now?*—in any circumstance—will expand your experience of love. For example, when you are in a situation where you feel so angry you want to explode, if you would just stop and ask yourself, *"What would love do right now?"* you will usually do something more loving than you would have done without asking the question. You may not do what Mother Teresa would have done, but you will do something more in alignment with who you really are. You will then be able to respond to life rather than react to it.

Asking w*hat would love do right now?* does not mean you will become a doormat and refrain from speaking up for yourself. In fact, just the opposite will occur. As you live from your heart and love yourself deeply, you will know when to stand up for yourself and perhaps say, *"No, I won't be doing that for you anymore," "That doesn't work for me,"* or *"That's unethical for me. I won't be joining you."* When you come from your natural essence, then speaking your truth will become second nature.

The more you ask *what would love do right now?* the more it will set you free to love again, to love completely, and to love from your heart without holding back. You can then be an example or model for others on how life can be extraordinary, fun, and expressive. Soon people may approach you and say, *"You are so different. You used to be so negative and crabby. How did you do it?"* They, and the people in their lives, will be so grateful if you take this opportunity to share with them your experience of asking, in any situation, *"What would love do right now?"*

When you feel love in your heart, you and everyone else benefits, because you have so much more love to give. It's all about making a real difference for you, your loved ones, and all those in your life who are willing to live from a powerful foundation of love.

As you use this book to evaluate your career, relationships, finances, health, and other areas of your life, you will begin to BE LOVE, rather than love being something toward which you are striving. Bring love to a situation and notice how others around you change, because you are different.

May the wisdom inside you take you on a journey into your heart where your greatness abides. ***Now, that's living a heart-centered, extraordinary life!***

What Would Love Do Right Now in Opening Your Heart?

Opening your heart fully may require courage to release resentment, animosity, or guilt associated with the past. It's really about accepting your humanity and the humanity of others.

In the following chapters, you will be engaging in the Inquiry to Resolution process as described in the Note to Reader section. When you complete each worksheet, the actions you create may include forgiving others for behavior that hurt you, or making amends to people you may have hurt. When taking these actions be sure you're in a safe situation before allowing yourself to be vulnerable.

This chapter looks at many approaches to forgiveness and what is involved in sincerely making amends.

Forgiveness

Freeing yourself from resentment and animosity toward others may be accomplished through forgiveness. There are many interpretations of what it is to forgive another.

My aha moment came when I read Doreen Virtue's *Forgiveness* card. I realized that forgiving someone doesn't mean what they did is okay, it simply means I'm no longer willing to hold onto any negative feelings in response to what happened—I don't have to forgive the action, just the person to be at peace.

In the PragerU.com video on forgiveness, Stephen Marmar explains that forgiveness is a very complex concept. He reviews three types of forgiveness: exoneration, forbearance, and release.

- **Exoneration** is when a person is truly sorry for hurting you and takes full responsibility (without excuses) for what they did, as well as assures you that they will not do it again—it wipes the slate entirely clean and restores the relationship.

- **Forbearance** is when an offender makes an inauthentic apology, or blames you somehow for causing them to behave badly. It leaves you with a degree of watchfulness yet cautiously optimistic, like *forgive but not forget* or *trust but verify*, and allows you to preserve relationships with people who, while far from perfect, are still important to you.

- **Release** is critically important for your well-being: it allows you to let go of what's weighing you down and eating away at your chance for happiness. It does not require that you continue the relationship, but like Doreen Virtue's concept, it asks that you let go of your bad feelings and preoccupation with the negative things that have happened to you.

Stephen Marmar concludes with, *"To forgive may be divine, but when we understand its dimensions we find that it is within our ability to do it."*

If you need an apology to forgive someone you're unable to locate, or who is deceased, write a letter from them to you and mail it to yourself. When you read it a few days later, imagine it's coming from the other person, allow yourself to receive the apology, and forgive them.

Forgiveness Specific to Child Abuse

Child abuse is one of the most difficult experiences to resolve, release, and heal. Some people assume the guilt and try, for many years, to forgive their abuser(s) without success, while others are determined not to forgive and are left living with the ongoing shame, pain, and hate without relief.

According to Bert Hellinger's philosophy of forgiveness—relative to children who have been psychologically, physically, or sexually abused—if a child forgives the abuser, in addition to the abuse the child suffered, the child will assume the guilt and responsibility for the abuser's behavior. Therefore, he insists that the child must *not* forgive the abuser. Based on Hellinger's philosophy, Magui Block's book, *Healing the Family*, presents a process through which abused children can heal themselves from the pain they've endured by giving the guilt and responsibility for the abusive behavior back to the abuser.

Four Steps to Making Amends

Making amends is about others and restoring those relationships that you have broken or damaged. The desire to make amends arises when you're willing to take responsibility for what happened and the impact it had on those involved. It's not suitable for everyday mishaps—it's best used for significant incidents that warrant extra consideration and may simply depend on the importance of the relationship.

When you harm others and make no effort to repair the relationship, you tend to avoid those people and large areas of your life become closed off. When you begin making amends, you have the opportunity to restore your relationships and have those areas open up again.

Seeking to mend a relationship involves forgiving yourself, offering a sincere apology, making necessary restitution, and accepting responsibility by taking steps to avoid making the same mistake in the future.

Step 1: Forgiving Yourself

Being able to make amends to others starts with forgiving yourself. In his *tiny buddha*® blog Michael Davidson says, *"Forgiving yourself is far more challenging than forgiving someone else, because you must live with yourself and your thoughts 24/7."*

When you've done something you consider wrong, the accompanying emotion registers in your nervous system. For example, you may feel guilty if you mistreated someone; or you may feel sad, if you made a mistake that cost you a friendship. When these emotions register, they usually contribute to negative thoughts and limiting beliefs you have about yourself, like *"I can't do anything right,"* or *"I'm a bad person."*

More than anything else, forgiving yourself requires that you acknowledge your actions have consequences for yourself and others. However, any attempt to forgive yourself—before letting go of the negative emotions and beliefs—won't work. You'll just continue to berate yourself, because your nervous system is in control.

I recommend using the Inquiry to Resolution process in this book to identify and release the limiting beliefs and negative emotions attached to the incident you want to heal in order to forgive yourself.

Step 2: Offering a Sincere Apology

In order for an apology to be effective, it must be genuine and go to the heart of the matter for the person you wronged. Consider carefully what you're going to say. Be accountable—don't make excuses or deflect blame. Be sure to include the crucial words, *I'm sorry.*

- State what happened.
  "I'm sorry I didn't pay you back when I promised I would."
- Acknowledge the impact your actions had on the other person to show that you fully understand.
  "I know it was my fault that you had to cancel your vacation."
- Express your desire to restore this relationship.
  "Our relationship means a lot to me."

Step 3: Making Restitution

Whether you've robbed someone of time, money, property, trust, attention, dignity, or well-being, it's important to do what you can to restore that which you've taken.

The essence of restitution is finding out what the other person needs and determining if, and when, you can provide that. It starts with an inquiry.

- Ask what the person needs from you to restore the relationship.

  "How can I make it up to you?"

Then, let the other person respond. Just listen. If the request is ethical and you're willing to fulfill on it, you have two options:

- Agree to their request and time frame.

  "I can do that when I get paid on Friday."

- Suggest an alternative if you're unable to comply.

  "I can't pay you in full now, but I will make weekly payments."

Step 4: Accepting Responsibility

Accepting responsibility is about making a genuine change in your behavior and taking on a whole new way of living.

Everyone has made mistakes, but the only mistakes that will undermine your happiness are the ones you're unwilling to admit.

Be honest in expressing what you've learned from this mistake. This helps the other person trust that you're sincerely making amends for your past behavior. Describe the ways in which you're making changes in your life to refrain from repeating the wrongdoing.

- Admit your transgression.

  "I was wrong to take your money and not honor my agreement."

- Tell what you've learned.

  "I've learned that I've been totally unreliable about money."

- Declare any action(s) you're taking.

  "I'm participating in a debt management course, and I'm having 10% of my paycheck directly deposited into a savings account."

Keep it simple. A long apology will start to lose its power. Make your points clearly and effectively.

Give the other person time to respond. Grant them the space, time, and freedom to vent, if necessary. Be willing to listen without judgment and accept their point of view, even if some of their perceptions of the situation seem inaccurate. They have every right to feel the way they feel.

Keep in mind, although making amends can free you, it doesn't always mean that the relationship will be restored—or that the process will be sufficient for the other person to forgive you.

In the Alcoholics Anonymous' 12-Step program, Step 9 states, *"Make direct amends to those people you have harmed wherever possible, except when to do so would injure them or others."* When direct amends are not possible or appropriate, there are many ways to complete the four-step process without personal contact. For example: you could write the person a letter; you could imagine yourself having a conversation with the other person; you could create a collage. Your mind does not know the difference between what is real and imagined, which is why visualization is so powerful.

You will be amazed how clean the slate becomes by making amends. Remember to be gentle with yourself throughout the process.

If someone is making amends to you, let them. Be generous and be gracious. Refrain from making the restitution you request out of proportion to what they did.

3

What Would Love Do Right Now in Your Formative Relationships?

As a newborn baby, you smell so good and feel so soft. You are kissable and huggable. You express yourself fully, holding nothing back. Even when you fill your diaper, others see it as an accomplishment.

Newborn babies are so miraculous. They are fresh, untouched, and unscathed by life, love, boys, girls, parents, school, other kids, or siblings. They are pure and precious. Each of us enters the world in this state.

So what happened? When does this begin to change for us? What happened is life in its fullest measure with all its giving and taking, its longings, disappointments, pleasures, pains, hurt, trauma, abuse, and even death. Over time, we become hardened, dry, unexpressive, angry, bitter, and mean; sometimes we even get abusive. You may not know any other way to be; you may take things out on others around you, especially those you love the most, and the cycle continues. You may be asking, *"Is this all there is? There has to be more to life than this." **I am here to tell you…there is!***

Your Relationship with Your Parents

Loving and being loved fully starts by healing your relationship with your parents. It's never too late, even if they are deceased or no longer in your life. Most of your current reality stems from unresolved past experiences while growing up with your parent(s) or primary caregiver(s).

As a young child, the world was all about you and you believed everything bad that happened was YOUR FAULT. For example: if your mother was crying, it was your fault; if your father was angry, it was your fault; if your parents divorced, it was your fault. As a result, you may have thought, *"If I were more helpful, my mother wouldn't be sad," "If I were quieter, my father wouldn't yell,"* or *"If I behaved better, they wouldn't get divorced."*

As a teenager, you may have shifted the blame to your parents believing every bad thing that happened to you was THEIR FAULT. For example: if your boyfriend broke up with you, it was somehow your mother's fault; if you didn't make the team, it was somehow your father's fault; if you failed your driver's test, it was somehow your parents' fault. As a result, you may have thought, *"There's something wrong with me," "I'm unlovable,"* or *"I can't count on anyone."*

As an adult, you may have come to understand that your parents did the best they could, and yet they were less than ideal parents. Like you, your parents were once children. They also experienced many unmet needs, disappointments, hurts, betrayals, and feelings that were never resolved. Like you, out of these unresolved experiences, they drew negative conclusions and developed beliefs about themselves, others, relationships, finances, and life in general, such as: *"I'm unworthy and don't deserve anything good," "Men hurt me/Women smother me,"* or *"Life is unsafe and scary."*

It's important to note that your parents behaved as if these conclusions, beliefs, and judgments were true—they could not be or act any other way—and neither can you.

However, if your inner child is still harboring feelings of hurt and betrayal, or any experiences of neglect, abandonment, or abuse, resolving them—putting them in the past where they belong—can free you to be the person you know you can be.

Completing the Inquiry to Resolution: My Relationship with My Parents is an opportunity to identify the earlier experiences, unresolved feelings, and conclusions you came to about yourself, others, and life that are currently keeping you from attaining the extraordinary life you are here to live. It is never too late to have a great relationship with your parents.

One incident relative to my relationship with my parents, which I healed, is revealed in the completed Inquiry to Resolution worksheet on the next few pages. It is designed to support you by illustrating what's possible by fully engaging in the process.

INQUIRY TO RESOLUTION
My Relationship with My Parents

INQUIRY (PAST)

1.	What incident happened between my parents and me, when I was growing up, that I want to heal?	*I am 11. I am shopping with my mom and two younger sisters for bathing suits. My mom says, "This year you can wear a two-piece swimsuit." Last year she insisted that I was TOO YOUNG! Finally! I am so thrilled until she also buys two-piece suits for my sisters who are ONLY 7 and 9.*
2.	How did I feel emotionally, mentally, physically, or spiritually at the time?	*Emotionally: I feel furious, angry, and betrayed. Mentally: I feel bewildered and confused. Physically: I feel tense and tight. Spiritually: I feel hopeless.*
3.	What, if anything, did I think about saying or doing that I didn't say or do in this situation?	*I hate you. Why do I have to obey all the rules and they don't? They should also have to wait until they're 11.*
4.	What did I conclude: ...about myself?	*I can't get what I want. What I want doesn't count. I am the experiment.*
	...about girls/women? ...about boys/men?	*Women are two-faced.*
	...about others (e.g., siblings, playmates, relatives, adults)?	*My mother is mean, strict, and doesn't care about what I want. My sisters don't have to live by the rules.*
	...about other areas of life (e.g., relationships, money, health)?	
	...about life?	*Once again, life is not fair.*

INQUIRY TO RESOLUTION
My Relationship with My Parents

RESOLUTION (PRESENT)

5.	How do the conclusions I drew and any feelings that I still hold (e.g., shame, blame, guilt, anger, envy, frustration, resentment, or regret) impact my life?	*I'm still holding on to anger, frustration, envy, and resentment. I find it difficult to ask for what I want, because I don't expect to get it, therefore I settle for less. I am envious of other people's ability to get what they want with ease.*
6.	What did I need emotionally, mentally, physically, or spiritually in this situation?	*Emotionally: I needed my mom to be consistent in applying her rules.* *Mentally: I needed her to clarify why the rules only seemed to apply to me.* *Physically: I needed to be the ONLY one getting a two-piece swimsuit.* *Spiritually: I needed to be honored and respected as the oldest.*
7.	In an ideal world, what could my parent(s) have said or done that would have made a positive difference for me?	*My mom could have said, "You look great in that two-piece swimsuit. You're growing up to be a beautiful young lady. I'm sure your sisters can hardly wait till they're old enough, too."*
8.	Drop down into your heart; breathe deeply; be open to love, compassion, and forgiveness; then let go using the instructions on the right.	Coming from love, say the following affirmation three times, while tapping your heart chakra (breastbone) with your fingers. *"I now release myself from the emotional, mental, physical, and spiritual effects of this incident and heal my heart."*
9.	How do I feel emotionally, mentally, physically, or spiritually now?	*Emotionally: Now I feel honored and respected.* *Mentally: Now I feel heard and validated.* *Physically: Now I feel calm and peaceful.* *Spiritually: Now I feel whole and centered.*

INQUIRY TO RESOLUTION
My Relationship with My Parents

ACTION (FUTURE)

Asking myself, *"What would love do right now?"*... I will take the following action(s) in my relationship(s) with those associated with this incident.	Date by which I will take this action.	✓
I will treat my mom with more compassion and kindness.	*Whenever we speak or see each other*	✓
I will make an appointment for my mom and me to enjoy a mani-pedi together.	*Within two weeks*	✓
I will take my mom to lunch at least once a month.	*1st of every month*	✓

Now it is your turn. Use the *Inquiry to Resolution: My Relationship with My Parents* worksheet available for download by going to my website at www.ExtraordinaryOutcomesPublishing.com/forms.

I invite you to answer the questions through the eyes of the child/teen/adult you were at the time of the incident. Let the emotions surface. They're inside you anyway. My philosophy is—better out than in. The more incidents you release and heal, the more freedom you will have to create an extraordinary life.

After completing this Inquiry to Resolution, you may notice how different you feel when you think of your parent(s). When you interact with them, they may appear more loving just because you did this process. If they are deceased or not present in your life, notice that you may feel more loving toward them—especially on Mother's Day or Father's Day.

Keep feeling. Keep breathing. Keep writing. As you do this process, you will begin to experience the very love and acceptance you have been longing to feel. When you complete this process, be sure to take some time to integrate what you've resolved.

Your Relationship with Others

While you were growing up, in addition to your relationship with your parent(s), your relationships with other people also continue to have an impact on how you relate to others in your day-to-day life.

Consider, as a child, there were moments in your relationships with your playmates/siblings when you may have felt jealous, superior, protective, rejected, shamed, etc. Also, you may have felt forced to interact and be on your best behavior with other family members—grandparents, aunts, uncles, cousins. During your school years, how your teachers and coaches related to you may have had a significant effect on your beliefs about your own intelligence, capacity to learn, and ability to compete. All of these relationships continue to affect how you relate to yourself and others, your self-confidence, as well as your view of life today.

Completing the Inquiry to Resolution: My Relationship with Others worksheet is an opportunity to identify these experiences and uncover the associations and limiting beliefs you developed that are keeping you from attaining the extraordinary life you are here to live.

One incident, involving my relationship with others, which I healed, is revealed in the completed Inquiry to Resolution worksheet on the next few pages. This example is designed to support you by illustrating what's possible by fully engaging in the process.

INQUIRY TO RESOLUTION
My Relationship with Others

INQUIRY (PAST)

1.	What incident happened between another person and me, when I was growing up, that I want to heal?	*I'm 14 at a family gathering in my father's hometown. My aunt takes one look at me and says—in front of everyone—"Oh my God, you're as white as a ghost. You look like a floozy. Who did your makeup? It looks horrible!"*
2.	How did I feel emotionally, mentally, physically, or spiritually at the time?	*Emotionally: I feel embarrassed, angry, and humiliated.* *Mentally: I feel attacked, confused, and shocked.* *Physically: I feel sweaty, flushed, and tense in my stomach area.* *Spiritually: I feel dirty somehow.*
3.	What, if anything, did I think about saying or doing that I didn't say or do in this situation?	*Mind your own business. You don't look so good yourself!*
4.	What did I conclude: ...about myself?	*I don't know what looks good. I'm not appropriate. I am an embarrassment. I can't get anything right. My best is not good enough.*
	...about girls/women? ...about boys/men?	*Women are jealous of me.*
	...about others (e.g., siblings, playmates, relatives, adults)?	*Relatives are "know-it-alls." People are mean and hurtful. People put me down in front of others.*
	...about other areas of life (e.g., relationships, money, health)?	*I can't trust those close to me.*
	...about life?	

INQUIRY TO RESOLUTION
My Relationship with Others

RESOLUTION (PRESENT)

5.	How do the conclusions I drew and any feelings that I still hold (e.g., shame, blame, guilt, anger, envy, frustration, resentment, or regret) impact my life?	*I'm still holding on to shame for wanting to look good. I consistently question if the choices I make are right and appropriate for the circumstances to ensure that I will never be publicly humiliated again.*
6.	What did I need emotionally, mentally, physically, or spiritually in this situation?	*Emotionally: I needed acknowledgment & love. Mentally: I needed not to be judged in public. Physically: I needed some hands-on tips for applying makeup suitable to my age. Spiritually: I needed compassion and understanding.*
7.	In an ideal world, what could the other person/people have said or done that would have made a positive difference for me?	*My aunt could have pulled me aside and said, "I notice you're wearing makeup now. You are turning into a beautiful young lady. If you want to, we can get together while you're in town, and I can give you some pointers about makeup so you can look even better."*
8.	Drop down into your heart; breathe deeply; be open to love, compassion, and forgiveness; then let go using the instructions on the right.	Coming from love, say the following affirmation three times, while tapping your heart chakra (breastbone) with your fingers. *"I now release myself from the emotional, mental, physical, and spiritual effects of this incident and heal my heart."*
9.	How do I feel emotionally, mentally, physically, or spiritually now?	*Emotionally: Now I feel special, cared for, & loved. Mentally: Now I feel guided and encouraged. Physically: Now I feel centered and serene. Spiritually: Now I feel beautiful and accepted.*

INQUIRY TO RESOLUTION
My Relationship with Others

ACTION (FUTURE)

Asking myself, *"What would love do right now?"*... I will take the following action(s) in my relationship(s) with those associated with this incident.	Date by which I will take this action.	✓
With forgiveness in my heart, I will send my aunt a card with current photos and an update about my life. I will let her know that I'm eager to hear about her life.	*Within the week*	✓
I will create a visual display celebrating my inner and outer beauty.	*Tomorrow night*	✓

The next few pages contain another completed Inquiry to Resolution worksheet involving my relationship with others, which I healed. It is designed to support you in examining those times when you hurt someone else.

INQUIRY TO RESOLUTION
My Relationship with Others

INQUIRY (PAST)

1.	What incident happened between another person and me, when I was growing up, that I want to heal?	*I am 13. Kevin leans over to kiss me. He opens his lips but not his mouth so I wind up kissing his teeth. It was wet and slobbery. I say, "Yuck! Where did you learn how to kiss?" I wipe his sloppy kiss off my mouth and he runs away.*
2.	How did I feel emotionally, mentally, physically, or spiritually at the time?	*Emotionally: I feel embarrassed, guilty, and shameful.* *Mentally: I feel mean.* *Physically: I feel flushed and my heart is racing. I want to run away and hide.* *Spiritually: I feel that I should do penance.*
3.	What, if anything, did I think about saying or doing that I didn't say or do in this situation?	*I thought about running after him and saying, "I'm sorry for being mean. You didn't deserve it. I overreacted. It was wrong of me. Is there anything I can do to make it up to you?"*
4.	What did I conclude: ...about myself?	*I'm mean, hurtful, and insensitive.* *I'm a bad person.*
	...about girls/women? ...about boys/men?	*Boys who are bad kissers are not for me.*
	...about others (e.g., siblings, playmates, relatives, adults)?	
	...about other areas of life (e.g., relationships, money, health)?	
	...about life?	

My Relationship with Others

RESOLUTION (PRESENT)

5.	How do the conclusions I drew and any feelings that I still hold (e.g., shame, blame, guilt, anger, envy, frustration, resentment, or regret) impact my life?	*I'm still holding on to shame, guilt, and regret. I go out of my way to make sure I am kind, considerate, and accepting of others—no matter what.*
6.	What did I need emotionally, mentally, physically, or spiritually in this situation?	*I needed to ease up on myself and realize that I made a mistake. I needed to give myself some compassion and understanding knowing I was still a good person. I needed an opportunity to apologize.*
7.	In an ideal world, what could the other person/ people have said or done that would have made a positive difference for me?	*Kevin could have said, "That was my first kiss, I have no idea what I'm doing. Do you want to try again?"*
8.	Drop down into your heart; breathe deeply; be open to love, compassion, and forgiveness; then let go using the instructions on the right.	Coming from love, say the following affirmation three times, while tapping your heart chakra (breastbone) with your fingers. *"I now release myself from the emotional, mental, physical, and spiritual effects of this incident and heal my heart."*
9.	How do I feel emotionally, mentally, physically, or spiritually now?	*Emotionally: Now I feel relieved and lovable.* *Mentally: Now I have the freedom to express myself with compassion.* *Physically: Now I can breathe easier.* *Spiritually: Now I forgive myself for being cruel.*

INQUIRY TO RESOLUTION
My Relationship with Others

ACTION (FUTURE)

Asking myself, *"What would love do right now?"*... I will take the following action(s) in my relationship(s) with those associated with this incident.	Date by which I will take this action.	✓
I'll do a visualization to make amends to Kevin for my behavior.	*This afternoon*	✓
I will practice self-forgiveness and compassion.	*Daily*	✓

Now it is your turn. Use the ***Inquiry to Resolution: My Relationship with Others*** worksheet at www.ExtraordinaryOutcomesPublishing.com/forms.

After completing this worksheet, you may notice how different you feel toward the people in your life. They may appear more caring and supportive. The more formative relationships you explore, release, and heal—the more freedom you will have to create an extraordinary life.

Keep feeling. Keep breathing. Keep writing. As you do this process, you will begin to experience the very love and affinity you have been longing to feel. When you complete this process, be sure to take some time to integrate what you've resolved.

What Would Love Do Right Now in Your Romantic Relationships?

A loving romantic relationship can be one of your most sacred experiences—as well as the most risky. Given the rewards, it is always worth the risk. I love the statement from Erica Jong's book, *How to Save Your Own Life*—"*Love is everything it's cracked up to be. That's why people are so cynical about it. It really is worth fighting for, being brave for, risking everything for. And the trouble is, if you don't risk anything, you risk even more.*"

My philosophy about intimate relationships is that when you make a commitment to love, everything unlike love arises to be released and healed.

Your reaction to what arises originates from unresolved issues, idealized concepts of romance, and conclusions you came to through observing your parents' relationship. Every romantic relationship you have will reflect and reinforce these issues, concepts, and conclusions until you release and heal them.

The healing available through the Inquiry to Resolution process is an opportunity for you to experience the very love you desire.

Your Parents' Relationship

Examining the relationship your parents had can provide insight into your experience of love and romance. How did they treat one another? Were they loving? Did they argue a lot? What was happening at significant ages while you were growing up? How did their relationship influence you?

As a child, you witnessed your parents' interactions and made decisions about romantic relationships based on those observations. We tend to have romantic relationships that are either just like our parents' or the exact opposite. For example, if your parents argued a lot, you may have decided that love is confrontational, so your relationships are tumultuous, violent, or chaotic. Perhaps one parent was weak and the other was domineering, so you decided the key to a winning relationship is to be equal in every way. Maybe your parents were overly affectionate, and you decided that a romantic partner must be lovey-dovey or they don't love you.

Remember in this process you are not pointing a finger at your parents or blaming them for the way your relationships turned out. You are identifying how YOU responded to what happened between them and the conclusions YOU came to about romantic relationships. The good news is, since you drew the conclusions—YOU can change them.

One incident from my parents' relationship, which I healed, is revealed in the completed Inquiry to Resolution worksheet on the next few pages. It is designed to support you by illustrating what's possible by fully engaging in the process.

INQUIRY TO RESOLUTION
My Parents' Relationship

INQUIRY (PAST)

1.	What incident did I witness between my parents, when I was growing up, that I want to heal?	*I am 11. My mother announces at a family meeting, "Your father and I are separating and he's moving out." We all start crying and asking questions. Mom orders us to calm down. My father says, "I don't want to move, but it's the best solution."*
2.	How did I feel emotionally, mentally, physically, or spiritually at the time?	*Emotionally: I feel sad, angry, scared, devastated. Mentally: I feel stunned and confused. Physically: I feel sick to my stomach. Spiritually: I feel helpless and alone.*
3.	What, if anything, did I think about saying or doing that I didn't say or do in this situation?	*No! Try harder. Work it out. What about us kids? Mom, if you weren't so bossy this wouldn't have happened. Dad, stand up for yourself! Why do you let her run all over you?*
4.	What did I conclude: ...about myself?	*I don't matter. My feelings and needs don't count. It must be my fault.*
	...about girls/women? ...about boys/men?	*Women are mean, insensitive, and overbearing. Men are weak and spineless.*
	...about others (e.g., siblings, playmates, relatives, adults)?	*Adults are selfish.*
	...about other areas of life (e.g., relationships, money, health)?	*Marriages don't work and they don't last.*
	...about life?	*Life isn't fair. I'll never get what I want and need. I'm doomed.*

INQUIRY TO RESOLUTION
My Parents' Relationship

RESOLUTION (PRESENT)

5.	How do the conclusions I drew and any feelings that I still hold (e.g., shame, blame, guilt, anger, envy, frustration, resentment, or regret) impact my life?	*I'm still holding on to blame, resentment, and guilt. I've been married and divorced two times. I assume committed relationships won't work, so I make sure I leave first to avoid being hurt.*
6.	What did I need emotionally, mentally, physically, or spiritually in this situation?	*Emotionally: I needed guidance and to know it wasn't my fault.* *Mentally: I needed clarity and to know my life would be the same.* *Physically: I needed to be held and reassured.* *Spiritually: I needed a healthy, loving family that gets along and resolves their differences.*
7.	In an ideal world, what could my parent(s) have said or done that would have made a positive difference for me?	*Mom could have said, "We love you. This isn't your fault. Everything is going to be alright. We know this is difficult and we're here for you." Dad could have reassured me, hugged me and said, "You'll be able to see and talk to me as much as you want. I'll always love you, whether we live together or not."*
8.	Drop down into your heart; breathe deeply; be open to love, compassion, and forgiveness; then let go using the instructions on the right.	Coming from love, say the following affirmation three times, while tapping your heart chakra (breastbone) with your fingers. *"I now release myself from the emotional, mental, physical, and spiritual effects of this incident and heal my heart."*
9.	How do I feel emotionally, mentally, physically, or spiritually now?	*Emotionally: Now I feel compassionate and open-hearted toward my parents.* *Physically: Now my body is relaxed and calm.* *Spiritually: Now I feel peaceful, centered, & loving.*

INQUIRY TO RESOLUTION
My Parents' Relationship

ACTION (FUTURE)

Asking myself, *"What would love do right now?"...* I will take the following action(s) in my relationship(s) with those associated with this incident.	Date by which I will take this action.	✓
I will make a donation to 4-H Clubs of America in memory of my father's long-time, commitment to volunteering for the organization.	*On his birthday every year*	✓
I will pay my mom's annual membership fee to New Frontiers, a senior organization, to support my mom's participation in the classes and social events she enjoys.	*Annually when it comes up for renewal*	✓

Now it is your turn. Use the ***Inquiry to Resolution: My Parents' Relationship*** worksheet at www.ExtraordinaryOutcomesPublishing.com/forms.

Keep feeling. Keep breathing. Keep writing. As you do this process, you will begin to experience how your parents' relationship influences the way you connect and relate with your romantic partners. When you complete this process, be sure to take some time to integrate what you've revealed. The more incidents you heal the more freedom you will have to create an extraordinary romantic relationship.

Your Romantic Relationships

Remember, you ARE love. Being LOVE is allowing yourself to be who you are and who you are not; and accepting your partner for who they are and who they are not. It isn't always easy. However, it is essential if you want to experience an intimate relationship beyond what you think is possible. Being love is the greatest gift you can bring to your relationship.

The concepts discussed in Chapter 1 of being present and getting gotten are particularly powerful in creating affinity and intimacy in romantic relationships. It's what has been so extraordinary in my relationship with my Beloved Bernie.

In the beginning of our relationship, Bernie understandably wanted to know about my past relationships. I told him, *"I'll share my past experiences with you, if you will celebrate who I've become as a result of healing my past and changing my old behaviors."* He lovingly said, *"Yes, I can do that."* This started a wonderful foundation of love and respect that continues to this day.

This is the first relationship I've ever been in where the love gets deeper and stronger and better over time, rather than worse. What's different? I'm different! I'm less serious, more playful, more patient, kind, understanding, and loving. I also take responsibility for my part in a situation sooner than I had done before. It can be very humbling at times, but always rewarding.

I'm much wiser now in relationship and we have a much better chance of a lifetime of happiness and fulfillment together, because of all my healing and growth from doing this work.

I've also let him know, he has the best me yet!

Developing a foundation of intimacy requires a willingness to tell your partner what's really going on with you; to care about what's going on with them; to share deep aspects of yourself—especially those things you don't want anyone else to know or ever find out—and to listen to them share things that you're not sure you want to hear.

Relationships are the only thing really happening. Everything is relational. You're in relationship with everything and everyone. Your intimate romantic relationship can be either a source of fun and pleasure or pain and suffering. To have extraordinary intimate relationships, it is essential that you heal wounds you're holding onto from past relationships.

One incident relative to an adolescent romance, which I healed, is revealed in the completed Inquiry to Resolution worksheet on the next few pages. It is designed to support you by illustrating what's possible by fully engaging in the process.

My Romantic Relationships

INQUIRY (PAST)

1.	What incident happened between another person and me that I want to heal?	*I am 12. I get on the bus and see my boyfriend, Tom, kissing my best friend, Cathy, on the cheek.*
2.	How did I feel emotionally, mentally, physically, or spiritually at the time?	*Emotionally: I feel angry. Under the anger, I feel betrayed, hurt, and embarrassed.* *Mentally: I feel confused.* *Physically: I feel sick to my stomach.* *Spiritually: I feel heartbroken.*
3.	What, if anything, did I think about saying or doing that I didn't say or do in this situation?	*How could you? You are both the scum of the earth. I don't want anything to do with either one of you!*
4.	What did I conclude: ...about myself?	*I am not good enough. I'm second best.*
	...about girls/women? ...about boys/men?	*Girls are disloyal and two-faced. Girls are out for themselves. I can't trust girlfriends.* *Boys are fickle. Boys cheat. Boys are dishonest. Boys are mean. I can't trust boys.*
	...about others (e.g., siblings, playmates, relatives, adults)?	
	...about other areas of life (e.g., relationships, money, health)?	*Relationships don't work.*
	...about life?	

INQUIRY TO RESOLUTION
My Romantic Relationships

RESOLUTION (PRESENT)

5.	How do the conclusions I drew and any feelings that I still hold (e.g., shame, blame, guilt, anger, envy, frustration, resentment, or regret) impact my life?	*I'm still holding on to resentment, blame, and betrayal. I don't expect those with whom I am in a relationship to be loyal. They always make something, or someone, more important than me.*
6.	What did I need emotionally, mentally, physically, or spiritually in this situation?	*Emotionally: I needed loyalty.* *Mentally: I needed honest communication.* *Physically: I needed comforting.* *Spiritually: I needed to be honored and respected.*
7.	In an ideal world, what could the other person/ people have said or done that would have made a positive difference for me?	*Cathy could have said, "I'm sorry I betrayed your trust and hurt your feelings." Tom could have said, "I'm such a jerk. I didn't take your feelings into consideration."*
8.	Drop down into your heart; breathe deeply; be open to love, compassion, and forgiveness; then let go using the instructions on the right.	Coming from love, say the following affirmation three times, while tapping your heart chakra (breastbone) with your fingers. *"I now release myself from the emotional, mental, physical, and spiritual effects of this incident and heal my heart."*
9.	How do I feel emotionally, mentally, physically, or spiritually now?	*Emotionally: Now I feel honored and respected.* *Mentally: Now I feel free from spite.* *Physically: Now I feel relieved.* *Spiritually: Now I feel compassionate.*

INQUIRY TO RESOLUTION
My Romantic Relationships

ACTION (FUTURE)

Asking myself, *"What would love do right now?"*... I will take the following action(s) in my relationship(s) with those associated with this incident.	Date by which I will take this action.	✓
I'll share with Bernie this resolved incident and discuss how my feelings about being betrayed in the past have impacted our relationship.	*This weekend*	✓
I'll write letters of forgiveness to Tom and Cathy, which I will release in a burning bowl ceremony.	*On the night of the next full moon*	✓

The next few pages contain another completed Inquiry to Resolution worksheet revealing a romantic relationship that I healed. It is designed to support you in examining those times when you hurt someone else.

INQUIRY TO RESOLUTION
My Romantic Relationships

INQUIRY (PAST)

1.	What incident happened between another person and me that I want to heal?	*I am 26. My husband has been away at school for 6 months. I am lonely. One night I run into an old friend, Tim, at the bar. He's paying a lot of attention to me. We're having fun dancing, drinking, and flirting. I start an affair with him that night.*
2.	How did I feel emotionally, mentally, physically, or spiritually at the time?	*Emotionally: I feel guilty, dirty, and scared.* *Mentally: I feel confused.* *Physically: My heart is pounding. I feel frozen.* *Spiritually: I feel disconnected and doomed.*
3.	What, if anything, did I think about saying or doing that I didn't say or do in this situation?	*No! I'm married. I'm not sleeping with you.* *I could have left the bar and gone home alone.*
4.	What did I conclude: ...about myself?	*I'm the scum of the earth.* *I'm damaged goods.* *I deserve to be punished.* *I'm not worthy of being loved.*
	...about girls/women? ...about boys/men?	*Men put their needs ahead of mine.*
	...about others (e.g., siblings, playmates, relatives, adults)?	
	...about other areas of life (e.g., relationships, money, health)?	*Breaking my marriage vow is OK.*
	...about life?	*Life is a struggle.*

INQUIRY TO RESOLUTION
My Romantic Relationships

RESOLUTION (PRESENT)

5.	How do the conclusions I drew and any feelings that I still hold (e.g., shame, blame, guilt, anger, envy, frustration, resentment, or regret) impact my life?	*I still feel genuine shame, guilt, and remorse about breaking my marriage vows. I withhold my sensuality to make sure I never do it again. I often feel the need to confirm with Bernie that our relationship is intact.*
6.	What did I need emotionally, mentally, physically, or spiritually in this situation?	*Emotionally: I needed to feel special and loved. Mentally: I needed to know that my marriage was solid, even in my husband's absence. Physically: I needed to experience intimacy. Spiritually: I needed to have compassion for my humanity.*
7.	In an ideal world, what could the other person/people have said or done that would have made a positive difference for me?	*Tim could have said, "It's been great spending time with you. We've had too much to drink. Let me get you a cab to take you home."* *I could have honored my vows, and gone home.*
8.	Drop down into your heart; breathe deeply; be open to love, compassion, and forgiveness; then let go using the instructions on the right.	Coming from love, say the following affirmation three times, while tapping your heart chakra (breastbone) with your fingers. *"I now release myself from the emotional, mental, physical, and spiritual effects of this incident and heal my heart."*
9.	How do I feel emotionally, mentally, physically, or spiritually now?	*Emotionally: Now I feel worthy to be loved. Mentally: Now I feel relieved. Physically: Now I feel calm and free. Spiritually: Now I feel centered and connected.*

INQUIRY TO RESOLUTION
My Romantic Relationships

ACTION (FUTURE)

Asking myself, *"What would love do right now?"*... I will take the following action(s) in my relationship(s) with those associated with this incident.	Date by which I will take this action.	✓
I forgive myself, then write a letter and make a vision board to complete my amends with my former husband.	*Within two weeks*	✓
I will share with Bernie what I discovered and healed that was holding me back from fully accepting his love for me.	*Tonight*	✓
I will create a spiritual retreat for myself to honor my humanity.	*Within a month*	✓

Now it's your turn. Use the **Inquiry to Resolution: My Romantic Relationships** worksheet available for download by going to my website at www.ExtraordinaryOutcomesPublishing.com/forms.

The more incidents you heal, the more light you will shed on how your patterns of behavior, feelings, and responses have impacted your experience of romantic relationships.

Regardless of your current romantic relationship status, completing this process is valuable in releasing any pain, loss, disappointment, betrayal, or rejection, so you can be fully present in your intimate relationships.

For those currently in an intimate romantic relationship, I recommend that each of you engage in this process; give yourselves plenty of time to heal; then share with each other what you discovered and released. This opens an opportunity for an authentic conversation with the partner you have about your needs, feelings, and desires.

Keep in mind your partner will also have unresolved hurts from the past. Be sensitive to your partner's experience. True intimacy in your relationship will be enhanced when these incidents are resolved. Do whatever is necessary to put the past in the past, where it belongs.

Keep feeling. Keep breathing. Keep writing. As you do this process, you will begin to experience the very love you have been longing to feel. When you complete this process, be sure to take some time to integrate what you've revealed.

5

What Would Love Do Right Now in Your Professional/Work Relationships?

Wherever you are right now in your career, business, or job is just that—it's where you are. You may be judging where you are by saying to yourself, *"I should be further along at this age. What went wrong?"* Each time you put yourself down, you stop the flow. Or perhaps you have the perfect job and you're thinking, *"I love my job and I hope it never changes."* Consider that change is inevitable and that this point of view may also stop the flow by preventing you from seizing new opportunities.

By examining what consistently occurs in your work life that blocks your path to success—being bypassed for promotion; harassed; treated unjustly; expected to take on every task offered; less than fairly compensated; or volunteering to do more than you can handle—you can then take action toward fulfilling your professional goals.

Along the way, you may also recall some negative messages you heard from your parents and influential adults in your life, like the following:

- *"To provide for your family and get a pension, you have to work for thirty years at the same job, even if you don't like it."*
- *"I didn't go to college. I'm not paying for you to go. Get a job."*
- *"Girls can't be doctors. / Boys can't be nurses."*
- *"The only way to make real money is to run your own business."*
- *"You're not talented enough to be in the movies."*

You are where you are because of the decisions you made based on limiting messages, past experiences, as well as unconscious conclusions and patterns. Identifying these decisions will help you understand why you are where you are today, and how they impact your work relationships with co-workers, bosses, employees, and clients.

A great way to discover your unconscious programming and where it came from is by completing the Inquiry to Resolution: My Professional/Work Relationships worksheet about your jobs, career, and business experiences.

One incident relative to my relationship with my first boss, which I healed, is revealed in the completed Inquiry to Resolution worksheet on the next few pages. It is designed to support you by illustrating what's possible by fully engaging in the process.

INQUIRY TO RESOLUTION
My Professional/Work Relationships

INQUIRY (PAST)

1.	What incident happened between my co-worker, boss, employee, etc., and me that I want to heal?	*I am 16. One day, after working 8 months at a drug store, my boss said, "We have to let you go." I said, "Where do you need me to go?" He replied, "Home—you're fired! Whenever you close, money is missing and the cash registers don't balance."*
2.	How did I feel emotionally, mentally, physically, or spiritually at the time?	*Emotionally: I feel stunned, shocked, devastated, betrayed, hurt, sad, scared, and helpless.* *Mentally: I feel numb, disoriented, and confused.* *Physically: I feel sick to my stomach, shaky, weak, and flustered.* *Spiritually: I feel despair.*
3.	What, if anything, did I think about saying or doing that I didn't say or do in this situation?	*How dare you accuse me of stealing money! I'm not the only one who uses these cash registers. You are making me pay for something I didn't do. Jerk!*
4.	What did I conclude: ...about myself?	*Doing my best isn't good enough. I'm powerless to defend myself. I'm not worth the benefit of the doubt.*
	...about girls/women? ...about boys/men?	*Men are arrogant and mean.*
	...about others (e.g., management, clients, owners, peers)?	*Bosses only care about themselves.*
	...about other areas of life (e.g., relationships, money, health)?	*It does not pay to work hard.*
	...about life?	*I'll never get ahead.*

INQUIRY TO RESOLUTION
My Professional/Work Relationships

RESOLUTION (PRESENT)

5.	How do the conclusions I drew and any feelings that I still hold (e.g., shame, blame, guilt, anger, envy, frustration, resentment, or regret) impact my life?	*I'm still holding on to shame, embarrassment, and resentment for being accused of stealing. I feel as though I must go above and beyond reasonable expectations in my business practices to prove I have impeccable integrity so my clients believe that I'm honest and trustworthy.*
6.	What did I need emotionally, mentally, physically, or spiritually in this situation?	*Emotionally: I needed compassion, guidance, and encouragement.* *Mentally: I needed clarity and understanding.* *Physically: I needed my boss to listen to me.* *Spiritually: I needed to be trusted and valued.*
7.	In an ideal world, what could the other person/ people have said or done that would have made a positive difference for me?	*He could have said, "Vicki, I know you're a very honest person, unfortunately I've noticed that on the nights you work and close the registers, they often don't balance. Let's go over how you're doing it and figure out what's happening."*
8.	Drop down into your heart; breathe deeply; be open to love, compassion, and forgiveness; then let go using the instructions on the right.	Coming from love, say the following affirmation three times, while tapping your heart chakra (breastbone) with your fingers. *"I now release myself from the emotional, mental, physical, and spiritual effects of this incident and heal my heart."*
9.	How do I feel emotionally, mentally, physically, or spiritually now?	*Emotionally: Now I feel acknowledged and supported.* *Mentally: Now I feel understood.* *Physically: Now I feel relaxed and calm.* *Spiritually: Now I feel hopeful.*

INQUIRY TO RESOLUTION
My Professional/Work Relationships

ACTION (FUTURE)

Asking myself, *"What would love do right now?"*... I will take the following action(s) in my relationship(s) with those associated with this incident.	Date by which I will take this action.	✓
I will visualize my old boss and acknowledge that he was just doing the best he knew how to protect his business.	*Right now*	✓
I will be more compassionate with myself and others.	*Daily*	✓
I will read "The Four Agreements," by Don Miguel Ruiz as a reminder to not take things personally.	*By the end of this month*	✓

Now it is your turn. Use the ***Inquiry to Resolution: My Professional/Work Relationships*** worksheet available for download by going to my website at www.ExtraordinaryOutcomesPublishing.com/forms.

Be extremely gentle with yourself at this point. If any limiting messages are still impacting your professional/work relationships, I recommend you complete an Inquiry to Resolution worksheet for each message.

Keep feeling. Keep breathing. Keep writing. After completing the process, you may begin to experience more rewarding work relationships, as well as being encouraged, acknowledged, respected, and honored. Be sure to take some time to integrate what you have revealed.

6

What Would Love Do Right Now in Your Health?

Health has many facets—physical, emotional, mental, and spiritual. Merriam-Webster defines health as "the condition of being sound in body, mind, or spirit." I define health as an expression of self-love resulting in a sense of vitality and overall well-being generated from within.

Many physical diseases today are a direct result of the unacknowledged and unexpressed emotions we harbor. In Louise L. Hay's book, *You Can Heal Your Life*, she identifies the mental thought patterns and emotions that correlate to different disease states and gives practical steps for releasing them through positive affirmations and forgiveness.

In this chapter, we will examine what would love do right now regarding your health. Pay special attention to the areas of nutrition, exercise, sleep, and rejuvenation.

Expressing Love For Yourself Through Nutrition

Our eating habits begin at home and are passed from one generation to the next. As children, we connect love with the eating customs with which we were raised—the rules around the table; the kinds of food we ate; the amount we consumed. We also form emotional and social eating habits throughout our lives, and may even subject ourselves to nutritional deprivation.

There are many philosophies about nutrition and food. Examine your current habits and begin identifying what you could do differently to make some improvements regarding your nutrition. You may want to do some research on the internet, try out different food plans, implement a cleansing regimen, or meet with a holistic nutritionist. Notice how you feel when you apply any changes. Use the ones that work for you, and leave the rest behind. You will discover what is best for you.

Through my own research, I found what's best for me is to eat whole, live, organic foods as much as possible. I do my best to eat fresh vegetables, lean meats, and fish. I also avoid GMO foods, carbonated beverages, and artificial sweeteners. One way I express love for myself is by drinking hot water with lemon, even in the summer, to help balance my pH level.

Expressing Love For Yourself Through Exercise

Exercise is also very important and can be of great benefit in leading a life of balance, happiness, and vitality. Exercising can include: walking, hiking, biking, swimming, lifting weights, or participating in classes, such as aerobics, yoga, Pilates, and dance. I invite you to take on identifying what you could do differently to express love for yourself through exercise. Again, research and experiment—you will discover what works best for you.

At this time in my life, the most rewarding physical activity that feeds my soul and my body is my morning 20-minute bike ride through the park. I love it!

Expressing Love For Yourself Through Sleep

Sleep is the time when your body regenerates itself. Research indicates that we need at least eight hours of uninterrupted sleep each day for our body to completely relax and recharge. Begin identifying what you could do differently to express love for yourself through better sleep. Perhaps create a before-bedtime routine that includes some relaxation—turn off the television, read something inspirational, journal what you are grateful for, and visualize what you're looking forward to having in the future.

To support uninterrupted sleep, I wear an eye mask and use earplugs to block ambient light and outside noise. My before-bedtime routine includes: not drinking water 1-2 hours before bedtime; reviewing what I've accomplished and am grateful for; thinking about the people who have touched my life and whom I have impacted during my day; and doing a short, guided meditation. I then easily drift off to a peaceful sleep.

Expressing Love For Yourself Through Rejuvenation

Everyone needs down time to restore, refresh, and renew their spiritual, emotional, and mental selves. People are re-energized in different ways; some by being alone, others by hanging out with friends; some by being in nature, others by dancing the night away; some by relaxing with a good book, others by playing board games; some by walking on the beach, others by volunteering at the local food bank; some by driving through the countryside, others by singing karaoke at the local bar; some by enjoying a fabulous spa day, others by tailgating at a football stadium. Begin identifying what you could do differently to express love for yourself through rejuvenation. Choose whatever suits your fancy—whenever, wherever, or however you please.

One of the things I do Monday evenings to feed my soul at every level is singing in the Higher Vibration Healing Choir at the Institute of Harmonic Science in Phoenix, AZ. This experience supports me in starting my week from a peaceful, serene, relaxed place; fills me with optimism, joy, and positive energy; and allows me to open my heart to the love that surrounds me.

A great way to distinguish your programming, regarding your health and well-being, and where it came from is by completing the Inquiry to Resolution: My Health worksheet.

One incident relative to my health, which I healed, is revealed in the completed Inquiry to Resolution worksheet on the next few pages. It is designed to support you by illustrating what's possible by fully engaging in the process.

INQUIRY TO RESOLUTION
My Health

INQUIRY (PAST)

1.	What incident happened in my life that I want to heal that is impacting a facet of my health?	*I am 7. My mother catches me hiding my peas under the edge of my plate and says, "Stop that. Eat everything on your plate. You should be grateful. There are starving children in China who would be happy to eat those peas. If you don't eat every single pea, you won't get dessert."*
2.	How did I feel emotionally, mentally, physically, or spiritually at the time?	*Emotionally: I feel annoyed and angry.* *Mentally: I feel confused and tricked into eating.* *Physically: I feel tense and sick to my stomach.* *Spiritually: I feel selfish and guilty.*
3.	What, if anything, did I think about saying or doing that I didn't say or do in this situation?	*I hate peas. Go ahead and send them to China, or eat them yourself. You're so mean.*
4.	What did I conclude: ...about myself?	*I'm selfish. What I want doesn't matter.*
	...about girls/women? ...about boys/men?	
	...about others (e.g., siblings, playmates, relatives, adults)?	*Adults are bossy and think they know what's best.*
	...about health and other areas of life (e.g., relationships, money, exercise)?	*Eating everything on my plate is a rule I have to obey.*
	...about life?	*I have to accept whatever I'm given. I have no control over my life.*

INQUIRY TO RESOLUTION
My Health

RESOLUTION (PRESENT)

5.	How do the conclusions I drew and any feelings that I still hold (e.g., shame, blame, guilt, anger, envy, frustration, resentment, or regret) impact my life?	*I'm still holding onto righteous indignation and lack of control. At home, I feel obligated to eat whatever Bernie buys rather than choose what I know is best for my health. When I eat out, I feel compelled to choose healthy options, and feel guilty when I order what I really want.*
6.	What did I need emotionally, mentally, physically, or spiritually in this situation?	*Emotionally: I needed compassion.* *Mentally: I needed to understand how eating food I hated was connected to other kids starving.* *Physically: I needed to be able to choose what I wanted to eat.* *Spiritually: I needed my food preferences to be respected.*
7.	In an ideal world, what could the other person/ people have said or done that would have made a positive difference for me?	*Mom could have said, "Tell me what you'd like to eat," and also included me in planning our family meals.*
8.	Drop down into your heart; breathe deeply; be open to love, compassion, and forgiveness; then let go using the instructions on the right.	Coming from love, say the following affirmation three times, while tapping your heart chakra (breastbone) with your fingers. *"I now release myself from the emotional, mental, physical, and spiritual effects of this incident and heal my heart."*
9.	How do I feel emotionally, mentally, physically, or spiritually now?	*Emotionally: Now I feel respected, heard, and acknowledged.* *Mentally: Now I feel clear and balanced.* *Physically: Now I feel relaxed.* *Spiritually: Now I feel peaceful.*

INQUIRY TO RESOLUTION
My Health

ACTION (FUTURE)

Asking myself, *"What would love do right now?"*... I will take the following action(s) related to my health.	Date by which I will take this action.	✓
I will go to the farmer's market and buy organic foods I like.	*2X per month*	✓
I will plan my meals ahead of time, so when I get hungry they are quick and easy to prepare.	*Every week*	✓
I will eat supper before 8:00 pm to support my digestion and health.	*Every day*	✓
I will donate money to the Hunger Project to support the creation of strategies for sustainable food production and the end of world hunger.	*Every month*	✓

Now it is your turn. Use the ***Inquiry to Resolution: My Health*** worksheet available at www.ExtraordinaryOutcomesPublishing.com/forms.

Review the areas related to your health. You could take one area and really go to work on it, or you could take an action in each category so all areas are improving and balancing at same time. Go with the flow. Notice the difference these improvements are making in your health and well-being. You will see and feel them and so will those around you. You will have more energy and enthusiasm to do the things that matter most.

Keep feeling. Keep breathing. Keep writing. After you do this process, you will begin to experience renewed vitality and well-being. When you complete the process, be sure to take some time to integrate what you have revealed.

7

What Would Love Do Right Now in Your Finances?

One of the most elusive aspects of life can be achieving financial abundance. Why do some people continually struggle, while others easily accumulate riches beyond what seems possible? Why do some people hoard their money, while others are generous to a fault? Why are some people driven to provide a large quantity of possessions, often at the expense of quality family time, while others have an expectation that everything will be provided for them without expending any effort?

In my coaching and counseling practice, some clients have shared their resentment that during childhood their parents always seemed to be working and never available to spend time with them. Other clients have reported that they are driven to provide financial stability for their families, at the expense of participating in family activities, which they regret—they just can't figure out how to do both.

One client who was unhappy and exhausted working 16 hours a day, six days a week, making a high six-figure salary, said, *"My father came home in just enough time to tuck me in and he was gone before I got up. Then on the weekends, he worked a second job."* In our session, she came to the realization, that like her father, she has to work hard all the time just to make a living—she has no choice. Using the Inquiry to Resolution process she examined her relationship to work and money, figured out what her choices were, and created the ideal job. She now lives a happy, balanced life making more money in fewer hours, doing work she loves, while spending plenty of quality time with her family.

How do you relate to money and the concepts of wealth, prosperity, and abundance? Do you have a balance that works well for you between making money and the other areas of your life?

We all grew up in a pervasive, cultural conversation about money. It's passed down from generation to generation; through our families, our communities, schools, the books we read, and the movies we watch. We're all familiar with some version of the following clichés:

The Classics:

- Time is money.
- Money is the root of all evil.
- Money can't buy happiness.
- A penny saved is a penny earned.
- Money makes the world go around.

There's Not Enough:

- We can't afford that.
- How are you going to earn it?
- There is no such thing as a free lunch.
- I'm not made of money.
- You have champagne taste on a beer budget.

Saving, Spending, and Debt:

- Save your money for a rainy day.
- Don't be penny wise and pound foolish.
- My money's burning a hole in my pocket.
- Rob Peter to pay Paul.
- Neither a borrower nor a lender be.

Show Me the Money:

- You have to work hard to make money.
- To make money, you have to spend money.
- Another day another dollar.
- Bring home the bacon.
- Buy low, sell high.

Rich vs. Poor:

- Wealthy people are greedy.
- Poverty is a virtue.
- Money is power.
- The rich get richer and the poor get poorer.
- Filthy rich and dirt poor.

Family Favorites:

- When I was your age, I didn't even get an allowance.
- Don't bite the hand that feeds you.
- A fool and his money are soon parted.
- Money doesn't grow on trees.
- You can't take it with you.

These phrases have been around for hundreds of years, they are entrenched in our culture, and part of our everyday life—we live as if this is the TRUTH about money. Is it any wonder that we continually struggle with our relationship to abundance and prosperity? Transcending how we relate to our beliefs about money, can allow each of us to easily accumulate riches beyond what seems possible today.

One incident relative to my finances, which I healed, is revealed in the completed Inquiry to Resolution worksheet on the next few pages. It is designed to support you by illustrating what's possible by fully engaging in the process.

My Finances

INQUIRY (PAST)

1.	What incident happened in my life that I want to heal that is impacting an aspect of my finances?	*I'm 17. I ask my mom about going to college and she says, "I can't afford to send you to college. You'll have to ask your father." I ask my dad and he says, "You're on your own for the 1st and 3rd years and I'll pay for your 2nd and 4th."*
2.	How did I feel emotionally, mentally, physically, or spiritually at the time?	*Emotionally: I feel angry, scared, and devastated. Mentally: I feel confused and unsupported. Physically: The pit of my stomach is tied in knots. Spiritually: I feel hopeless and alone.*
3.	What, if anything, did I think about saying or doing that I didn't say or do in this situation?	*Mom, I've been cleaning YOUR house and helping raise YOUR kids, since I was 12. I've even been working to buy my own clothes, and you haven't thought enough about me to save for my future. Dad, I need your help now, not later. I've proved I'm responsible. I get good grades. I have a job. I take care of your other children. What more do I have to do to get your love and support?*
4.	What did I conclude: ...about myself?	*I'm on my own. I'm not worth helping. I'll never make it. I have to figure things out by myself.*
	...about girls/women? ...about boys/men?	*Women are selfish and self-absorbed. I have to prove myself to men.*
	...about others (e.g., siblings, playmates, relatives, adults)?	*My own father doesn't believe in me. No one cares about me. I can't get any support from anyone.*
	...about money and other areas of life (e.g., relationships, work)?	*Money is scarce. I have to pay my own way.*
	...about life?	*Life is unpredictable and scary.*

INQUIRY TO RESOLUTION
My Finances

RESOLUTION (PRESENT)

5.	How do the conclusions I drew and any feelings that I still hold (e.g., shame, blame, guilt, anger, envy, frustration, resentment, or regret) impact my life?	*I'm still holding on to anger and resentment. I don't consult with anyone about my finances and have no budget. I pay my expenses in full each month, but severely limit discretionary spending. I save for retirement, but not for emergencies. I have no assets and avoid being in consumer debt.*
6.	What did I need emotionally, mentally, physically, or spiritually in this situation?	*Emotionally: I needed acknowledgment, appreciation, and validation.* *Mentally: I needed guidance and counsel.* *Physically: I needed financial support.* *Spiritually: I needed encouragement and love.*
7.	In an ideal world, what could the other person/people have said or done that would have made a positive difference for me?	*My mother could have said, "I'm so grateful for everything you've done to help me here at home, I would gladly send you to college if I had the money. Let's get together with your father and make a plan." My father could have said, "I'm proud of your academic accomplishments and appreciate how hard you work. I'd be honored to pay your college tuition."*
8.	Drop down into your heart; breathe deeply; be open to love, compassion, and forgiveness; then let go using the instructions on the right.	Coming from love, say the following affirmation three times, while tapping your heart chakra (breastbone) with your fingers. *"I now release myself from the emotional, mental, physical, and spiritual effects of this incident and heal my heart."*
9.	How do I feel emotionally, mentally, physically, or spiritually now?	*Emotionally: Now I feel honored, respected, & loved.* *Mentally: Now I feel focused and confident.* *Physically: Now I feel relieved and relaxed.* *Spiritually: Now I feel connected and supported.*

INQUIRY TO RESOLUTION
My Finances

ACTION (FUTURE)

Asking myself, *"What would love do right now?"*... I will take the following action(s) regarding my finances.	Date by which I will take this action.	✓
I will find a financial planner to support me in creating my financial future.	*Within 30 days*	✓
I will use the information provided by my financial planner to make wise choices regarding my retirement.	*Within 2 months*	✓
I will implement a comprehensive monthly budget including a savings plan based on my current income and expenses.	*This month*	✓

Now it is your turn. Use the ***Inquiry to Resolution: My Finances*** worksheet available at www.ExtraordinaryOutcomesPublishing.com/forms.

This is the opportunity to examine your life experiences about money that are blocking your path to the financial future of your dreams. I suggest paying particular attention to those incidents from which you drew conclusions about scarcity/abundance; spending/saving; giving/receiving; debt/financial planning; and being rich/poor. When you identify the financial blocks in your life, you're halfway there. You can then take action toward the fulfillment of your financial goals.

Keep feeling. Keep breathing. Keep writing. As you do this process, you will begin to experience a new relationship to prosperity and abundance. When you complete the process, be sure to take some time to integrate what you have revealed.

8

What Would Love Do Right Now in Your Self-Expression?

W hen you are self-expressed, you live life from the essence of who you are without much attention on yourself. You are so present in the moment, being who you are, that your inner critic is silenced, the constant flood of thoughts, ideas, and opinions in your mind slows down, and you're fully alive just doing your thing—whether that be dancing, playing guitar, making love, hiking in nature, expressing your truth with another, meditating in communion with your divine self, or simply being grateful for your life.

This chapter will examine what love would do right now regarding your self-expression in the areas of creativity, communication, and spirituality.

Accessing Your Self-Expression Through Creativity

As you move into having a more balanced life, be sure you're honoring all the areas of life that are important to you—work, family, hobbies, friends, education, relationship, and remember to include creativity. Give yourself permission to take an art class, learn gourmet cooking, make some furniture, write a travel blog, re-build a classic car, design a new landscape—whatever stirs your creativity. It is essential to embrace the very things that spark your passion to support you in living a more meaningful, satisfying, fun, and fully self-expressed life.

I found a way to access my own creativity when I realized my life was totally out of balance. Although I was highly successful and *living the dream,*

I felt disconnected, overwhelmed, frustrated, and exhausted.

Several years ago, I felt like my entire life was doing-doing-doing, work-work-work, focus-focus-focus—always having to be in charge, on task, totally responsible, no breaks, no opportunity to have some fun and express any other part of myself.

One day it occurred to me that in my twenties I loved dancing at the great clubs in Chicago, and perhaps learning to ballroom dance now could provide the opportunity to permit someone else to be in charge—my partner would do the leading and I would be able to relax and follow. When I started taking lessons, I tapped into my innate ability to create balance, go with the flow, unwind, and allow fun in my life again. I opened myself to something new and discovered the freedom to be my true self. Within six months, I was making new friends, meeting the love of my life, traveling, participating in local dance competitions—winning in every category. I was also more passionate about my connection with my clients and excited about expanding my business. Although I no longer compete, I still enjoy expressing my creativity through country and ballroom dancing.

Accessing Your Self-Expression Through Communication

Anything can be resolved in communication. Withholding communication or not speaking your truth may show up in your body, affect your clarity of mind, shape your emotional well-being, and impact your spiritual connection. Taking responsibility and letting other people know what is really going on with you can resolve conflict, deepen intimacy and closeness, and free you to be truly connected with others.

Honoring yourself, speaking your truth, and expressing your natural way of being includes asking powerfully for what you need, voicing your wants, desires, and longings, letting others know what you will and will not do, and honestly answering yes or no when others ask you to do something.

One very powerful communication principle is to take responsibility—in the moment—for how you perceive challenging situations. It's not always easy when you're emotionally activated to take ownership for your attitude, words, and actions—however, doing so can deepen your relationship with others.

An effective method I have used to express responsibility in my communication is what I call a *do-over*.

One day Bernie walked through the door right after I had a frustrating conversation with the phone company. I was very angry and snapped at him as he came in the door. I immediately knew that was not how I wanted to greet him, and he didn't deserve that. So, I paused and took a deep breath and said, *"I am so sorry for blasting you when you came in. I am really glad you are here. Can we have a do over? If you could please go back outside and return in about two minutes, I will greet you from the love I have for you in my heart."* He answered, *"Sure."* He left, came back in and said, *"Hi, honey, how are you doing?"* I replied, *"Hi, honey, it's great to see you. Actually, I just got off the phone with the phone company and I am very angry right now. I need a few more minutes to cool off so I can get back to normal and really be with you."* He responded, *"Okay, no problem; if you want my input about the phone company, I'd be glad to help you."* I said, *"Thanks."* I took five minutes and when I came out, I was able to listen to his perspective, it turned out to be one I could embrace and apply. The rest of my time with Bernie that evening was delicious and delightful. The icing on the cake was getting a different response the following day when I called the phone company back. Coming from my heart instead of my head made a noticeable difference.

Accessing Your Self-Expression Through Spirituality

How does spiritual self-expression relate to love?

I believe awakening your spirituality begins with self-love—accepting yourself exactly as you are—having compassion for your weaknesses and celebrating your gifts—expressing the natural love of self with which you were born.

One of the highest spiritual expressions you can offer is loving others the way they are and the way they are not, and allowing yourself to be loved in return—this is unconditional love.

Feeling whole and complete within yourself, you can then love others from the overflow. You can expand your capacity to love by keeping your heart open no matter what—honoring yourself—expressing your needs and desires—and tapping into your uniqueness. Doing this will naturally spill over to those you love and can be an inspiration to those who love you. You can then encourage each other to be authentic and bring your unique self-expression to all your relationships and all areas of life.

One of the ways I connect to my inner divinity is to ride my bicycle through the park and sing *I Love Myself the Way I Am*, written by Jai Josephs.

I love myself the way I am,
there's nothing I need to change.
I'll always be the perfect me,
there's nothing to rearrange.
I'm beautiful and capable,
of being the best me I can.
And I love myself, just the way I am.

I love you the way you are,
there's nothing you need to do.
When I feel the love inside,
it's easy to love you.
Behind your fears, your rage and tears,
I see your shining star.
And I love you, just the way you are.

I love the world the way it is,
'cause I can clearly see.
That all the things I judge are done,
by people just like me.
So 'til the birth of peace on earth,
that only love can bring.
I'll help it grow, by loving everything.

I love myself the way I am,
and I still want to grow.
But change outside can only come,
when deep inside I know.
I'm beautiful and capable,
of being the best me I can.
And I love myself, just the way I am.

Accessing your self-expression—through exploring specific events in your life and the impact they had on your creativity, communication, and spirituality—can bring you more joy, peace of mind, happiness, fulfillment, and love.

Three incidents—one in each area—which I healed, are revealed in the completed Inquiry to Resolution worksheets on the following nine pages. They are designed to support you by illustrating what's possible by fully engaging in the process. The first incident involves my creativity.

INQUIRY TO RESOLUTION
My Self-Expression

INQUIRY (PAST)

1.	What incident happened in my life that I want to heal that is impacting my creativity?	*I'm in 4th grade. I'm reading my wonderful report about my family's camping trip to the class and everyone is laughing. I don't know why they're laughing at me. I return to my seat in tears. My teacher calls on the next student.*
2.	How did I feel emotionally, mentally, physically, or spiritually at the time?	*Emotionally: I feel hurt, embarrassed, betrayed, and shattered.* *Mentally: I feel confused and perplexed.* *Physically: I feel nauseous, tearful, and frozen.* *Spiritually: I feel disconnected and alone.*
3.	What, if anything, did I think about saying or doing that I didn't say or do in this situation?	*Stop it, why are you being so mean to me? This is a great story what's wrong with you?* *Mr. King, aren't you going to stand up for me and stop them? What kind of a teacher are you?*
4.	What did I conclude: ...about myself?	*I'm insufficient. My ideas are worthless.*
	...about girls/women? ...about boys/men?	*Girls are critical and cruel.* *Boys are mean and nasty.*
	...about others (e.g., siblings, playmates, relatives, adults)?	*Teachers are uncaring and don't help me.*
	...about other areas of life (e.g., communication, creativity, spirituality)?	*It's not safe to share my writing with anyone. I can't voice my own ideas and opinions. It's too risky to be myself.*
	...about life?	*Life is dangerous.*

INQUIRY TO RESOLUTION
My Self-Expression

RESOLUTION (PRESENT)

5.	How do the conclusions I drew and any feelings that I still hold (e.g., shame, blame, guilt, anger, envy, frustration, resentment, or regret) impact my life?	*I'm still holding on to embarrassment. I've written 7 books and it has taken me 5 years to get even the first one published, because I think it has to be perfect or no one will like it. I'm afraid to speak in public about myself, my life, and my books.*
6.	What did I need emotionally, mentally, physically, or spiritually in this situation?	*Emotionally: I needed validation and encouragement.* *Mentally: I needed understanding and support.* *Physically: I needed applause.* *Spiritually: I needed acceptance and sensitivity.*
7.	In an ideal world, what could the other person/ people have said or done that would have made a positive difference for me?	*The class could have given me a standing ovation and said, "That was great. You really brought it to life. I never knew camping could be so much fun. I want to go on vacation with you next year."*
8.	Drop down into your heart; breathe deeply; be open to love, compassion, and forgiveness; then let go using the instructions on the right.	Coming from love, say the following affirmation three times, while tapping your heart chakra (breastbone) with your fingers. *"I now release myself from the emotional, mental, physical, and spiritual effects of this incident and heal my heart."*
9.	How do I feel emotionally, mentally, physically, or spiritually now?	*Emotionally: Now I feel elated and admired.* *Mentally: Now I feel confident and self-assured.* *Physically: Now I feel calm, open, and energized.* *Spiritually: Now I feel accepted and celebrated.*

INQUIRY TO RESOLUTION
My Self-Expression

ACTION (FUTURE)

Asking myself, *"What would love do right now?"*... I will take the following action(s) related to my self-expression.	Date by which I will take this action.	✓
I will publish my first book.	*Within 2 months*	✓
I will promote my book and my business at a minimum of one speaking engagement or book signing per month.	*Beginning 1 month after publication*	✓
I will hire an internet-marketing specialist to launch my book to #1 Bestseller status on Amazon.com.	*1 week after publication*	✓

The next incident, which I healed, is relative to my communication.

INQUIRY TO RESOLUTION
My Self-Expression

INQUIRY (PAST)

1.	What incident happened in my life that I want to heal that is impacting my communication?	*I am 4. We live in an apartment above our landlady. I'm playing and running around the house. My mom yells, "Be quiet. Stop running. You'll get us thrown out." I say, "No! I'm having fun." She says, "Don't talk back, just do as you're told."*
2.	How did I feel emotionally, mentally, physically, or spiritually at the time?	*Emotionally: I feel angry.* *Mentally: I feel confused.* *Physically: I am pouting.* *Spiritually: I feel crushed.*
3.	What, if anything, did I think about saying or doing that I didn't say or do in this situation?	*As I cry and stomp my feet, I yell, "You can't make me. I'm telling Daddy when he gets home that you're being mean to me."*
4.	What did I conclude: ...about myself?	*I'm naughty and bad.*
	...about girls/women? ...about boys/men?	
	...about others (e.g., siblings, playmates, relatives, adults)?	*Adults are mean and no fun.*
	...about other areas of life (e.g., communication, creativity, spirituality)?	*I'm not allowed to say or do what I want.*
	...about life?	*I have to do what I'm told.* *I have to be a good girl.* *I have to make my mom happy.*

INQUIRY TO RESOLUTION
My Self-Expression

RESOLUTION (PRESENT)

5.	How do the conclusions I drew and any feelings that I still hold (e.g., shame, blame, guilt, anger, envy, frustration, resentment, or regret) impact my life?	*I'm still holding on to frustration. I don't speak up. I learn and follow the rules. I settle for less than what I really want. I don't rock the boat. I accommodate other people's needs.*
6.	What did I need emotionally, mentally, physically, or spiritually in this situation?	*Emotionally: I needed compassion.* *Mentally: I needed to understand.* *Physically: I needed to be comforted.* *Spiritually: I needed acceptance.*
7.	In an ideal world, what could the other person/ people have said or done that would have made a positive difference for me?	*My mom could have stopped what she was doing, put me on her lap, lovingly explained to me why I needed to be quiet and not run in the house, and then read a book to me.*
8.	Drop down into your heart; breathe deeply; be open to love, compassion, and forgiveness; then let go using the instructions on the right.	Coming from love, say the following affirmation three times, while tapping your heart chakra (breastbone) with your fingers. *"I now release myself from the emotional, mental, physical, and spiritual effects of this incident and heal my heart."*
9.	How do I feel emotionally, mentally, physically, or spiritually now?	*Emotionally: Now I feel calm and loved.* *Mentally: Now I feel understood.* *Physically: Now I feel relaxed.* *Spiritually: Now I feel accepted and valued.*

INQUIRY TO RESOLUTION
My Self-Expression

ACTION (FUTURE)

Asking myself, *"What would love do right now?"*... I will take the following action(s) related to my self-expression.	Date by which I will take this action.	✓
I will practice saying yes when I mean yes, and no when I mean no.	*Daily*	✓
I will have a session with my holistic practitioner to release my belief that I can't have what I want.	*Within two weeks*	✓
I will buy a coloring book and crayons and scribble outside the lines using all the wrong colors.	*This weekend*	✓

The third incident, which I healed, is relative to my spirituality.

INQUIRY TO RESOLUTION
My Self-Expression

INQUIRY (PAST)

1.	What incident happened in my life that I want to heal that is impacting my spirituality?	*I am 11. Shortly after my confirmation in the Catholic church, my parents separate. My father moves out of the house. I pray every day, with all my heart, for God to bring my daddy home. My father doesn't come home.*
2.	How did I feel emotionally, mentally, physically, or spiritually at the time?	*Emotionally: I feel sad and betrayed.* *Mentally: I feel bewildered.* *Physically: I feel anxious.* *Spiritually: I feel angry at God and hopeless.*
3.	What, if anything, did I think about saying or doing that I didn't say or do in this situation?	*You promised that you would answer my prayers. Where the hell are you? Why won't you help me? What am I supposed to do now?*
4.	What did I conclude: ...about myself?	*I don't matter. I'm not heard. I'm not worthy.*
	...about girls/women? ...about boys/men?	
	...about others (e.g., siblings, playmates, relatives, adults)?	
	...about other areas of life (e.g., communication, creativity, spirituality)?	*I don't trust God to be there for me, ever.*
	...about life?	*I'm doomed. I'm alone and on my own.*

INQUIRY TO RESOLUTION
My Self-Expression

RESOLUTION (PRESENT)

5.	How do the conclusions I drew and any feelings that I still hold (e.g., shame, blame, guilt, anger, envy, frustration, resentment, or regret) impact my life?	*I often feel unsupported. I rarely ask for what I really want, because I never expect to get what I ask for and therefore settle for less than I want. When I do ask for something and I don't get it, I feel angry and frustrated.*
6.	What did I need emotionally, mentally, physically, or spiritually in this situation?	*Emotionally: I needed to feel loved.* *Mentally: I needed certainty that my prayers would be answered.* *Physically: I needed my dad to come home.* *Spiritually: I needed to trust in God's promise to guide and care for me.*
7.	In an ideal world, what could the other person/people have said or done that would have made a positive difference for me?	*God could have answered my prayers. My father would move home and my parents would have lovingly resolved their differences and demonstrated the possibility of honoring their vows and commitment to being a family.*
8.	Drop down into your heart; breathe deeply; be open to love, compassion, and forgiveness; then let go using the instructions on the right.	Coming from love, say the following affirmation three times, while tapping your heart chakra (breastbone) with your fingers. *"I now release myself from the emotional, mental, physical, and spiritual effects of this incident and heal my heart."*
9.	How do I feel emotionally, mentally, physically, or spiritually now?	*Emotionally: Now I feel worthy to be loved.* *Mentally: Now I feel relieved.* *Physically: Now I feel calm and free.* *Spiritually: Now I feel hopeful and connected.*

INQUIRY TO RESOLUTION
My Self-Expression

ACTION (FUTURE)

Asking myself, *"What would love do right now?"*... I will take the following action(s) related to my self-expression.	Date by which I will take this action.	✓
I'll make a list of the things I want that I haven't been asking for and start asking for them.	*This week*	✓
I will ask my friends to help Bernie and me deep clean, declutter, and organize our living environment to my satisfaction.	*Schedule within two weeks*	✓
I will create a spiritual retreat for myself.	*Within a month*	✓

Now it is your turn. Use the ***Inquiry to Resolution: My Self-Expression*** worksheet at www.ExtraordinaryOutcomesPublishing.com/forms.

So, what would love do right now in your self-expression? Explore the areas of creativity, communication, and spirituality as they relate to your self-expression. You could take one area and really go to work on it, or you could work on all of them.

Keep feeling. Keep breathing. Keep writing. As you do this process, you will begin to experience more ease in expressing yourself and creating a more balanced life. When you complete the process, be sure to take some time to integrate what you have revealed.

9

What Would Love Do Right Now in Restoring Your Power?

A loss of personal power often occurs when you have what is called a triggered response. This happens when you are going along great in life, then someone comes too close, says or does something unexpected, you see/hear/ smell something, and—BAM—you have an emotional reaction that feels out of proportion and/or inappropriate relative to what just happened. These triggers call up negative or hurtful experiences from the past, which impact your feelings, thoughts, and behaviors in the present. Your response can be big or small, immediate or sneak up on you slowly—it usually comes from traumatic, upsetting, unresolved, or suppressed memories. When you are reacting in this way, you have less power to be present and take appropriate action.

Since I have introduced Bernie to the question, what would love do right now, when he notices I'm triggered he reminds me to use it. He simply looks into my eyes and says, *"Honey, what would love do right now?"* That brings me to the present and I say, *"Oh, love would relax and take a deep breath. I'm going to take some time right now to figure out what this is all about. See you in a bit."* He kindly replies, *"I'll be here when you're finished. Let me know if you need anything from me."* Then I use the Restoring My Power process to explore the incident that triggered me, release the past, and heal my heart.

I recommend you do this for yourself when you are triggered. It will set you free to love again. It will also set others free. I was able to resolve one of my recurring upsets triggered by Bernie's behavior, through inquiring into what caused it, then choosing to make my needs a priority, and restoring my power.

I used to get quite angry and feel disrespected on the many mornings that Bernie left a mess in the kitchen before going to work. When I examined what bothered me so much about it, I remembered the first time my mom got home from work before I had cleaned the house to her strict standards. She started yelling, *"I can't believe you didn't do what I asked. You are so ungrateful. I work hard to keep us in a nice neighborhood."* I concluded right then that being accepted depended on knowing the rules and obeying them to the letter, and that people who don't clean up after themselves are ungrateful slobs. I was then able to share with Bernie in a new way. I let him know what I had discovered about the rules I have for being socially acceptable, and how I saw his behavior as being disrespectful and dishonoring me, whenever he left a mess in the kitchen. This provided us with the opportunity to lovingly work together to express our needs and desires and create a plan that worked for both of us.

The Restoring My Power process has two parts. Step 1 is to complete a Recognizing My Triggers worksheet, and Step 2 is completing an Inquiry to Resolution worksheet relative to the corresponding incident.

On the next page is a completed Recognizing My Triggers worksheet revealing one trigger from my life, which I healed. It is designed to support you by illustrating what's available by fully engaging in the process.

RECOGNIZING MY TRIGGERS
RECOGNIZING MY TRIGGERS
Restoring My Power

INCIDENT

1.	What happened that triggered a response in me that was out of proportion and/or inappropriate?	*I've been an ultrasound tech for 18 years. I have a work injury preventing me from doing my job. My doctor says, "You're just being fragile like a China Doll, I think you're exaggerating your pain level to get out of going back to work. So, I'm closing your Workman's Compensation case."*
2.	What was my mental, emotional, physical, or spiritual response when I was triggered?	*Emotionally: I feel furious, frantic, and terrified. Mentally: I feel panic and think I'm going to die. Physically: I'm trembling, my heart is pounding. Spiritually: I feel abandoned and helpless.*
3.	What, if anything, did I say or do that was out of proportion to what happened in this situation?	*I said, "How dare you call me a liar! You cannot possibly know my level of pain. I'm in excruciating pain all the time. If you close my case and I lose the job I love, I'll report you to the medical board." I slammed the door on my way out of his office.*
4.	What, if anything, did I think about saying or doing that I didn't say or do that was out of proportion to what happened in this situation?	*Why in the world would I avoid going back to work? I want to go back to work. As a highly-skilled, 18-year Medical Ultra-sonographer who was highly paid, I'm now having to live on a Worker's Comp stipend, which is 1/8 of my salary. Are you nuts? You jerk. Watch me! I will not let you undermine my career!*
5.	What corresponding incident does this remind me of from the past?	*It reminds me of the time I was wrongly accused of stealing money from the cash registers and was fired from my first job, working at the drug store.* (See my Inquiry to Resolution: Profession/Work worksheet in Chapter 5.)

Now it is your turn. Use the **Recognizing My Triggers: Restoring My Power** worksheet and the corresponding **Inquiry to Resolution** worksheet available at www.ExtraordinaryOutcomesPublishing.com/forms.

You may notice the work you've completed in previous chapters is already reducing how often you are triggered and what triggers you. You may be aware of having more energy, being more peaceful, or experiencing more happiness.

Keep feeling. Keep breathing. Keep writing. As you do this process, you will begin to be more powerful in the face of challenging people and situations. When you complete the process, be sure to take some time to integrate what you have recognized and resolved.

10

What Would Love Do Right Now in Designing Your Life?

Here's your opportunity to step into being the chief executive officer of your life. As the CEO creating your extraordinary life, what would you do differently? How would you talk to yourself? What inner positive qualities would you express?

Consider that the first and most important person in your life is you. You may be concerned that putting yourself first is selfish. It's actually the opposite—it's very empowering. Loving yourself and doing what's best for you, is best for those you love and those who love you.

When doing the exercises in this chapter, don't hold anything back, keep asking, *"What would love do right now?"* Let the part of you that knows, reveal the inner desires that come from your heart. You can apply everything you've healed so far to clarify your purpose and design your ideal day, ideal home life, ideal career, and ideal relationship—the life you've always wanted.

This process will reveal a lot. You'll be amazed. You may see where you're settling for what you think you should be doing, according to family traditions and cultural norms, rather than having what you really want in life.

You may experience being blocked, not having clarity, or unable to even imagine what you want. If you're stuck, don't worry, I recommend looking at the areas of life and relationships discussed previously and completing an Inquiry to Resolution process to open yourself to living a life by design.

For those engaged in this process with a partner, it's important to share what you're each discovering. Your revelations could be a huge turning point in your relationship and your life together. For example, you might be living in the desert, but both of you really want to live near the beach.

I recommend after completing each exercise that you create a physical or virtual display, called a vision board, using various images from magazine clippings to photographs and keepsakes. This display is designed to motivate your creativity and support the manifestation of what you want. Studies show that defining and visualizing what you want to accomplish is more powerful than wishing and waiting for something to happen (Mapping Perception to Action in Piano Practice: Harvard, 2003).

Vision boards are especially fun to create with others. For example, create a vision board with your family that depicts a fabulous vacation you've always wanted to take and put it up on the fridge; or with your partner design a trendy bathroom remodel and hang it on the mirror; or with your teenagers create amazing summer activities and post their vision boards in their bedroom— imagine teaching your sons and daughters how to manifest what they want throughout their lives, at such an early age—the possibilities are endless.

As you declare your purpose and ideals, you may discover actions you want to take immediately. Ultimately, you will naturally take inspired actions toward fulfilling your aspirations, which will move you closer to manifesting your extraordinary life.

Clarifying Your Purpose

I believe each of us is born with a purpose. As children, we suppress our sense of purpose in order to be accepted and fit in. We stop expressing our heartfelt desires and forget who we were born to be. There are those who never realize their purpose. They simply live their lives defined by what they're taught at home, in school, or at their place of worship.

What would it be like to live a purpose-filled life? Those magical moments when you are fully engaged—in the flow, losing track of time, on a roll, on top of the world—are unconscious expressions of your purpose. Once you are present to your purpose, you can live a life filled with magical moments.

Do you wake up and do the same things every day like in the movie *Groundhog Day*—get up, shower, shave, get dressed, eat breakfast, go to work, go to the gym, stop at the store, pick up the dry cleaning, return home, eat, watch TV, play with the kids, and go to bed? Then, the next day, you do it all over again—asking yourself, *"What's the point?"*

By clarifying your purpose, life can take on a completely new meaning—it can truly be an adventure, whatever you're doing. Purpose is more than what you're doing—it's a way of being that you bring to life, such as love, inspiration, or a desire to bring out the best in others. It can be as far-reaching as ending world hunger or as personal as putting food on your family's table.

It is so important to know that what you identify as your purpose is enough—it is right for you right now. Comparing your innate purpose with anyone else's is futile. You may think someone else's purpose is grander than yours—it's not—each person's purpose is distinct. Your goal is to be fully yourself, the best possible you, and let your light shine.

I clarified my purpose by examining my life through a series of powerful questions adapted from the *Raised Vibration Owning My Purpose Workshop*™.

- Which behaviors did I give up and which do I still use to survive?
- In what areas am I fulfilled, contented, or dissatisfied?
  - Relationships
  - Career
  - Health
  - Finances
  - Self-expression
  - Personal Power
- What principles guide my personal behavior and actions?
- What am I doing when I'm in the zone and lose track of time?
- What am I passionate about? / What makes my heart sing?

DESIGNING MY LIFE
My Purpose

CREATE IT!

In reviewing my life, I realized that by the time I turned 5, I had given up my curiosity, sense of adventure, and playful nature in order to be a "good girl," help with my siblings, obey the rules, and please my mom.

The older I became, as more demands were made of me, I found it necessary to give up my authenticity, as well as my full self-expression. Over time, I abandoned my desires and passions, even my dignity, and became accommodating, agreeable, and submissive to foster harmony within the family and get approval, acknowledgment, and acceptance.

In the workshop, as I evaluated the areas of my life that were working and not working, I recognized a reawakening of my desires and passions through my spiritual connection, my relationships, and my career—all of which were very fulfilling. I was satisfied with my health and finances. However, in the areas of my personal power and full self-expression, I remained accommodating, agreeable, and submissive to maintain harmony and acceptance.

The facilitator then had us focus on identifying core principles. I distinguished mine as love, inspiration, empowerment, encouragement, as well as honor and respect. Next, I reflected on being in the zone. I noticed that I tend to lose track of time when I am engaged in heart-felt conversations, creative writing, and being alone in nature. These exercises culminated in discovering that I am passionate about people living extraordinary lives.

*At the end of the workshop when asked, "What way of being lights you up—what is your purpose?" My answer was clear—**I inspire and empower others' greatness to live extraordinary lives.***

*Since my life is continually evolving, I periodically review my purpose. I recently realized that I hadn't included myself, so I created a new version with a few more details—**I inspire and empower myself and others to live extraordinary lives overflowing with love, adventure, passion, and joy!***

DESIGNING MY LIFE
My Purpose

ACTIONS

Asking myself, *"What would love do right now?"*... I will take the following action(s) to move toward living consistent with my purpose.	Date by which I will take this action.	✓
I'll participate in fun, adventurous and/or playful activities.	*Weekly*	✓
I will be in communication with my partner, family, friends, and clients.	*Consistently*	✓
I will discuss how I can support others in living a life filled with love, adventure, passion, and joy.	*Frequently*	✓

My new Vision Board.

I inspire and empower myself and others to live extraordinary lives overflowing with love, adventure, passion, and joy!

Now it's your turn. Have fun. Be creative. Use the **Designing My Life: My Purpose** worksheet at www.ExtraordinaryOutcomesPublishing.com/forms.

Your purpose is the foundation for the design of your ideal, extraordinary life and impacting the lives of the people around you, through whatever you are doing. Therefore, I recommend clarifying your purpose before moving on.

Designing Your Ideal Day

Living consistent with your purpose, what would your ideal day look like from the moment you wake up until your head hits the pillow at night?

The power of designing your ideal day is that it pulls you into action consistent with what you say you want. Now is the time to playfully create your ideal day—with no limits on time, money, location, or obligation. What would it look like, feel like, be like? Are you alone or with others; working, playing, relaxing, vacationing; are you happy, joyful, grateful, loving, peaceful; is it creative, productive, inspiring, easygoing; does it align with your purpose?

What new strategies and options can you implement? What and/or whom might you need to let go of or bring into your life? What do you need to learn, do, create, or release to have your ideal day be your reality? What is the future you want to live into?

I created my ideal day by examining the following five questions:

- What am I doing?
- When am I doing it?
- Who's with me?
- Where am I?
- How do I feel?

DESIGNING MY LIFE
My Ideal Day

CREATE IT!

I wake up at six o'clock, after eight hours of uninterrupted sleep, happy, refreshed, and ready for a new adventure. There is a gentle breeze and the sun is shining through the open window in my spacious, well-lit home overlooking a tropical beach. I put on a lightweight, cotton sundress over my swimsuit, then putter for about half an hour, while enjoying a glass of fresh-squeezed orange juice. Before heading out for a long, energizing walk on the beach to my favorite writing spot, I gather up my writing pad, a pen, a protein drink, a wide-brimmed hat and my sunglasses.

When I come to the peaceful, secluded cove where the waves gently lap along the white, sandy beach, I sit down, get comfortable, finish my protein drink, and spend the next hour expressing my passion through writing. If the download is flowing, I stay even longer.

I joyfully return home and find my beloved Bernie in the shower, I eagerly join him and afterwards we put on soft, romantic music and make love.

Later we get dressed and eat a delicious, organic garden salad for lunch. Then, Bernie goes to work and I walk down the hall to my office where I support my clients in creating their extraordinary lives.

After Bernie gets home at six o'clock, I prepare dinner while he goes for a walk. We have a delightful and delicious meal of fresh fish, wild rice, and organic vegetables. Around eight o'clock, we go to our favorite coffeehouse, have dessert with close friends, and listen to some live, acoustic music.

We return home and sit quietly on the deck holding hands, stargazing by the light of the moon. At ten o'clock I crawl into bed; Bernie comes in to snuggle; after a few minutes, he leaves to have some alone time; then I drift off to sleep feeling loved, grateful, and fulfilled.

DESIGNING MY LIFE
My Ideal Day

ACTIONS

Asking myself, *"What would love do right now?"*... I will take the following action(s) to move toward manifesting my ideal day.	Date by which I will take this action.	✓
Make sure I'm in bed every night by 10 pm.	*Tonight*	✓
Devote at least an hour every morning to my writing.	*Within 2 weeks*	✓
Manage client appointments to accommodate my schedule.	*Within a month*	✓
Set aside time at least three evenings per week to participate in social activities with Bernie and my friends.	*Next week*	✓

Now it's your turn. Have fun. Use the ***Designing My Life: My Ideal Day*** worksheet at www.ExtraordinaryOutcomesPublishing.com/forms.

Designing Your Ideal Home Life

Living consistent with your purpose, what would your ideal home life look and feel like? Your physical environment is integral to how you experience living in your home. It is where you go for respite and rejuvenation. A home is often a reflection of the thoughts and beliefs of the individuals living there. I notice that when my home is cluttered, my mind is scattered.

I created my ideal home life by examining the questions below:
- Where would I like to live?
- What kind of house do I want?
- Who is living with me?
- Am I working from home?
- How would I decorate my home?
- How would my home be organized?
- What would I experience living in this environment?

DESIGNING MY LIFE
My Ideal Home Life

CREATE IT!

My beloved Bernie and I live in a beautiful 3,000sf four-bedroom, plantation-style home that sits on a tropical peninsula overlooking a private, white, sandy beach. A flowing set of stairs descends casually down to the water's edge providing access for our long, romantic walks at sunset. We enjoy breathtaking ocean views from the lanai that wraps around the house.

Our floor plan is arranged according to feng shui principles. From the entrance, our master bedroom is intentionally located in the far-right corner of the home to nurture our intimate, harmonious relationship. My home office, with a separate client entrance, is strategically situated in the far-left corner to enhance my healing practice, support my creative writing, and promote financial abundance.

The kitchen opens to the great room with its magnificent, panoramic view of the ocean. It has a large island, polished white quartz countertops, birchwood cabinets, and white appliances. The great room has 14-foot cathedral ceilings; reclaimed teak hardwood floors; room for an exquisite, hand-crafted dining room table that expands to seat up to sixteen; and soft, comfortable leather furniture for relaxing and entertaining guests.

From his on-site executive studio, Bernie advertises and manages our two, tiny-house, short-term, vacation rentals located on our lush, meticulously landscaped, three-acre estate. We employ a full-time groundskeeper and a housekeeper who live in a quaint, little casita set back from the main house, surrounded by a lovely, organic vegetable garden. There is also a three-car garage with an adjacent, fully-equipped workshop where Bernie repurposes flea-market finds and donates them to homeless shelters.

My life and my home are organized—there's a place for everything and everything's in its place. Each room has its own eclectic character and is tastefully decorated. All of our personal and financial affairs are in order, allowing us to really enjoy each other's company, deepening our intimacy.

Our home provides the environment for relaxation and rejuvenation. Bernie and I are very happy and continue to support each other's greatness as we enhance the lives of others who enter our home.

DESIGNING MY LIFE
My Ideal Home Life

ACTIONS

Asking myself, *"What would love do right now?"*... I will take the following action(s) to move toward manifesting my ideal home life.	Date by which I will take this action.	✓
Visit a variety of tropical coastal countries to evaluate options and financial viability for living on the beach.	*This year*	✓
Continue to purge unnecessary household items to declutter our home and simplify relocation.	*Every week*	✓
Prepare our current home and guest house to be separate, short-term rental properties for additional income.	*Within nine months*	✓
Hire a Certified Financial Planner to support me in creating a life of financial freedom.	*Within one month*	✓

Now it's your turn. Use your imagination. Use the ***Designing My Life: My Ideal Home Life*** worksheet available for download by going to my website at www.ExtraordinaryOutcomesPublishing.com/forms.

Designing Your Ideal Profession/Work

Living consistent with your purpose, how could you express it through your ideal profession/work over the next year? five years? ten years? This is a great opportunity to evaluate how you use your work-related time, and then create what you really want.

The U.S. Department of Labor reports that adults spend over 50% of their waking time working or in work-related activities. This includes running a business, gainful employment, homemaking, volunteering, and pursuing your profession through education.

People spend much of their time at work being unhappy and unfulfilled. According to reports by Business Insider from various sources:

- The average person spends 90,000 hours at work over their lifetime;
- 80% of people are dissatisfied with their jobs;
- 25% of employees say work is their main source of stress and 40% say their job is, *"very or extremely stressful."*

Doing work that is fulfilling and rewarding can contribute to happiness, contentment, and the experience of inner peace. Marsha Sinetar presents a philosophy that inspired me in creating my ideal career, in her book, *Do What You Love and the Money Will Follow* (Dell Publishing, 1987).

Keeping my declared purpose in mind—*I inspire and empower myself and others to live extraordinary lives overflowing with love, adventure, passion, and joy*—and answering the questions below, I realized that although I chose a career that called to me and I love the work I do, something was missing. I used this exercise to authentically design my ideal profession.

- Do I enjoy what I'm doing now?
- What do I really love doing?
- How do I want to make a difference?
- How do I want to express my natural talents and skills?
- What work environment do I want (e.g., employed/self-employed, work alone/on a team, work indoors/outdoors)?

DESIGNING MY LIFE
My Ideal Profession/Work

CREATE IT!

I am joyfully and gratefully making a huge difference in the lives of others, fulfilling my purpose—I inspire and empower myself and others to live extraordinary lives overflowing with love, adventure, passion, and joy!

I am a best-selling author, speaker, transformational healer, and coach in high demand for my expertise and wisdom. I am thriving in my business, Center for Extraordinary Outcomes, which is dedicated to the expansion of people's greatness and their capacity to manifest a life they love! I have the profound joy to be a part of the miracles they create.

Many people seek out my intuitive skills and talents to access their innate wisdom in order to identify, clear, and heal the unconscious patterns that hold them back from having what they want in life. Through my ability to listen powerfully, be fully present and non-judgmental, my clients feel safe during sessions to enter the alpha state of consciousness where deep healing and transformation occur.

From my ideal home overlooking the ocean, I serve three clients per day, three days a week; I lead one repatterning group each month; and have the profound pleasure to conduct three transformational workshops per year to enthusiastic participants; all coordinated by my fabulous support team that serves my every need and are at my beck and call, allowing me to focus on making a difference without distraction. This ideal schedule affords me the luxury of traveling one week each month, with my Beloved Bernie, for fun and adventure.

My Extraordinary Outcomes Publishing company also has an awesome team of experts facilitating the process—from manuscript to print—with ease and grace. The question, what would love do right now, posed in my first best-selling book, goes viral—impacting people globally. I am sought after for radio and TV interviews, speaking engagements, and book signings. Every year I write and publish another best-seller, which Oprah eagerly reads and endorses to her book club members.

DESIGNING MY LIFE
My Ideal Profession/Work

ACTIONS

Asking myself, *"What would love do right now?"*... I will take the following action(s) to move toward manifesting my ideal profession/work.	Date by which I will take this action.	✓
Hire a marketing specialist and create a campaign to generate referrals.	*Within 1 month*	✓
Schedule time with social media experts to create the best strategies for my business.	*Within 2 weeks*	✓
Schedule one book signing per month.	*Begin next month*	✓
Develop a workshop based on my book, ***What Would Love Do Right Now?***	*Within 4 months*	✓

Now it's your turn. Have fun. Be creative. Use the **Designing My Life: My Ideal Profession/Work** worksheet available for download by going to my website at www.ExtraordinaryOutcomesPublishing.com/forms.

Designing Your Ideal Relationships

Living consistent with your purpose, what would your ideal relationships be like? There are many different types of relationships from familial to friendship, neighbor, co-worker, and romantic partner. Consider designing your ideal relationships in each area of life where you are relating to others.

I created my ideal romantic relationship by exploring these three questions:

- What do I need in my relationships in order to thrive?
- What do I want/desire to be happy/satisfied in my relationships?
- What boundaries must be respected/maintained?

I recommend using these same questions when designing all of your ideal relationships.

DESIGNING MY LIFE
My Ideal Relationships

CREATE IT!

I have a mutually beneficial, fulfilling, committed relationship with the man of my dreams. We share common interests and are spiritually compatible. I love him with an open heart and it is returned to me tenfold. I feel accepted, desired, respected, cherished, and adored by him. When our eyes meet, we share a profound knowing of our love for one another, which often moves us to tears.

We experience open communication, divine tenderness, unconditional trust, encouragement, and support as best friends. We honor our differences and resolve conflicts as they occur so our hearts are available to receive even more love and compassion. I am always safe to express my true feelings.

We share a deep and abiding understanding that we would never intentionally do anything to hurt the other. The language of love that feeds my soul is affirmation—receiving love notes, cards, and flowers when I least expect it. I revel in providing what my partner needs that enhances our enduring commitment. We enjoy soothing massages, long embraces, cuddling on the couch, and spooning in bed—which culminates in intense sexual passion and mutual fulfillment.

We thrive living together in harmony and anticipating the delight of reuniting after a gratifying, purpose-filled day's activities. He is genuinely funny and his clever wit makes me spontaneously laugh out loud. We enjoy cooking savory and delicious meals together and exploring new culinary dishes and fine wines from different parts of the world. Our conversations are rich and relaxed. We toast to our good fortune and sacred companionship.

We are financially free, enjoy robust health, and love traveling to exotic locations around the world visiting historic sites, immersing ourselves in different cultures, and walking barefoot on tropical beaches. We stroll through open-air markets admiring the skill of local artisans. We experience grace and ease with each other and the charming people we meet along the way.

Our foundation and expression of love models and inspires what's possible for others in intimate relationships.

DESIGNING MY LIFE
My Ideal Relationships

ACTIONS

Asking myself, *"What would love do right now?"*... I will take the following action(s) to move toward manifesting my ideal relationships.	Date by which I will take this action.	✓
I will ask Bernie what language of love feeds his soul. I will also clarify with him what I need that feeds my soul.	*This weekend*	✓
I will invite Bernie to reread with me our commitment vows to strengthen the foundation of love we share.	*Within a week*	✓
I will plan and participate in fun activities with Bernie and our friends.	*Weekly*	✓
I will resolve any conflict or miscommunication with Bernie.	*ASAP*	✓

Now it's your turn. Follow your heart. Use the ***Designing My Life: My Ideal Relationships*** worksheet available for download by going to my website at www.ExtraordinaryOutcomesPublishing.com/forms.

Now that you've clarified your purpose and designed your ideals, it's time to start living your extraordinary life. Continue to ask yourself, *"What would love do right now?"* Let the answers be your guide.

Here is the vision board I created to manifest my ideal relationship, career, and things that are most important to me: fun, romance, passion, prosperity, publishing this book, celebration, travel to tropical beaches, golf, adventure, and being a sought-after speaker who inspires people to create extraordinary lives.

When I view this vision of my ideal future:
I shift from wishing it could happen—to declaring it will happen.
I shift from dreaming how it might be—to affirming how it will be.
I shift from hoping it will turn out—to knowing that it will manifest.
I shift from waiting for it to come to me—to proclaiming it is mine.

11

What Would Love Do Right Now in Living Your Extraordinary Life?

In this chapter, you will apply all of the work you've done to enhance your life and relationships, by writing three personal manuals—Guide to Daily Living, Guide to Romantic Intimate Relationship, and Guide to Sexual Satisfaction—as declarations of who you are in the world and how you want to be treated by others.

Guide to Daily Living

This personal manual is designed to support you in declaring what works for you in your daily interactions with the people in your life—what you like and don't like; how you expect to be treated; and how you intend to treat others. Consider the various areas of your life: from family, to work, to play, to community, to...

Guide to Romantic Intimate Relationship

This personal manual is your opportunity to design all of the things you desire in your most important relationship, and how you thrive in partnership.

Guide to Sexual Satisfaction

This personal manual expresses to your partner how he/she can love and satisfy you sexually.

If you are currently in a romantic relationship, I recommend that you ask your partner to also complete and share all three of their personal manuals, so together you can have a deeper experience of the love you feel for each other to create a mutually beneficial and enduring partnership.

For those who are not currently in a romantic relationship, I suggest clarifying your expectations and preferences by completing these Guides. After distinguishing what you desire, you may notice how optimistic and ready you are for the love of your life to seemingly appear out of nowhere.

I have provided my completed Guides on the next several pages to support you by illustrating what's available by fully engaging in the process. For me, this process was both daunting to contemplate and freeing to complete. While I was writing my personal manuals, I knew how valuable it would be for Bernie to do the same as a way to deepen and expand our relationship and honor our love. I delivered my invitation with the heartfelt love letter on the next page. He was moved by my commitment to our partnership and graciously accepted my invitation to provide his manuals.

Dear Beloved Bernie,

The most valuable gift I can possibly give you is a manual on how to love and satisfy me. I am doing this because you mean so much to me and I know you want to please me. My manual reveals all the ways you can win and succeed in loving me. I would love it if you would also let me know the best way to love you so we can more deeply experience our profound and abiding love.

Right now, I am loving you the best way I know how, which is the way I like to be loved. I look forward to discussing our innermost desires, expectations, and acknowledgments so that we can better understand who we truly are, what we genuinely want, and how to live together harmoniously and create our fabulous future.

There is no better time for openness and revealing our inner longings. I know we can contribute to the world as a model for love between couples, by continuing to share what we are learning and experiencing together. What an opportunity to make a difference!

Of all the people in the world, I choose you. Thank you for loving me. I am who I am today, because of your love for me.

I love you dearly!

Victoria

LIVING YOUR EXTRAORDINARY LIFE
Guide to Daily Living

PERSONAL MANUAL

Alone Time	*I take time each morning to connect with my divine nature through my spiritual practices of meditation, yoga, reading, puttering, walking/riding my bike in the park, all to align with my intentions for the day.*
Communication	*Kindness rules! I consider how my words and actions might impact others and expect others to do the same in return. I value clarity. I say what I mean, and I mean what I say. I do my best to provide honest and open communication with the people in my life. Whenever a miscommunication occurs between us, I appreciate the opportunity to resolve any conflict or misunderstanding in a timely manner.*
Creative Self-Expression and Hobbies	*I sing at the Higher Vibrations Healing Choir. I go dancing every chance I get. I write books. I create my Dazzle Your Dangles™ earring holders with a group of women who meet to work on art and craft projects.*
Forms of Acknowledgment	*I'm a hugger. I enjoy greeting my friends with a hug. I make a point to remind my friends how much they mean to me, and I love it when they tell me how much I mean to them. I enjoy sending cards of acknowledgments, bestowing special gifts of appreciation, and treating friends to dinner. I love it when friends reciprocate and surprise me with their unique forms of acknowledgment.*
Friendship	*My friends are the people in my life who make me a better person. I love that they are happy for me and support my greatness. I have fun and spend quality time with them frequently. I value the intimacy and the feeling of being safe to openly share about our lives, being exposed to different perspectives, and exchange loving observations and reflections with each other.*

LIVING YOUR EXTRAORDINARY LIFE
Guide to Daily Living

PERSONAL MANUAL *(cont'd)*

Having Fun	*I love picnicking, kayaking, sitting on the beach, golfing, dancing, attending concerts/spiritual events, watching a good movie, or reading a great book.*
Health and Self-Care	*I take the necessary supplements to heal my body and maintain its youthful appearance. I receive massages and facials, acupuncture, chiropractic sessions, physical therapy, an annual women's wellness visit, and transformational healing sessions to rejuvenate myself and support my health.*
Humor and Laughter	*While I tend to take life too seriously, I love to laugh. I deeply appreciate when others make me laugh out loud by adding genuine humor to everyday situations. I also like to watch romantic comedies.*
Integrity	*Integrity to me means keeping my word—honoring what I say I'll do by when I say I'll do it—and when I'm unable to do what I promised, I communicate immediately and make a new promise, and I expect the same from the people in my life.*
Lifestyle	*Being respected, honored, and accepted for who I am and who I am not are paramount. I prefer being in a committed relationship. I'm a morning person. I love cooking, being outdoors, and traveling to exotic beach locations often. I enjoy my healing work with clients as well as creating and working on projects to accomplish the extraordinary outcomes I want in my life.*
Making a Difference in the World	*In alignment with my purpose: I support the Hunger Project; I contribute by sharing the wisdom of my life experiences and professional training to a global audience through my books; and I live my life from my philosophy of, what would love do right now?*

LIVING YOUR EXTRAORDINARY LIFE
Guide to Romantic Intimate Relationship

PERSONAL MANUAL

Creating Our Future	*I need to know that my partner and I share a common vision of our future together. I require a detailed, written action plan to support manifesting the future we've designed together. I want to factor in accountability by scheduling time each month to track our progress and maintain momentum.*
Quality Time	*It is very important to me to spend time with my partner free of distractions, chores, deadlines, or interruptions. We have fun going to interesting places and doing interesting things, with interesting people... or intimate getaways with just the two of us.*
Spiritual Time	*I connect with my divine nature daily and need a partner who is in alignment with my spiritual path and participates in spiritual group experiences and regular Sunday services.*
Transition Time	*When I come home from work, I prefer to spend at least 15 minutes alone to shift my focus from my clients to my partner, followed by time together to share our day.*
Leisure Time	*I have a strong desire to travel to exciting places and experience new cultures. My partner and I will take two long vacations to tropical beaches every year, and one getaway weekend each month.*
	I love to dance, go to the movies, the theater, and festivals, see tribute bands, hike local trails, go out for fabulous meals—and I take real pleasure doing all the things I do for fun with my partner.
	My partner and I host other couples in our home for intimate dinners and playing cards or board games.
	I occasionally like to watch major sporting events.

LIVING YOUR EXTRAORDINARY LIFE
Guide to Romantic Intimate Relationship

PERSONAL MANUAL *(cont'd)*

Family Time	*My partner and I take pride in our home, maintaining it as an open and welcoming place for all family members to visit. In addition, we enjoy participating in various entertaining activities and excursions—in or out of town—with family.*
	It's also important to me that I honor my mother's request to spend time alone with her each month.
Being Cherished	*I love surprises that demonstrate affection and admiration. They stop me in my tracks and bring me back to the present moment so I can savor the gift of love. I love hearing the words, "I love you" and seeing them in print on love notes that turn up in places where I least expect them. I adore receiving live plants, a dozen long-stemmed crimson red roses, and tickets to special events. My favorite surprise is to be whisked away in a stretch limo for a romantic weekend. My partner showers me with gifts he knows I will enjoy.*
Touch and Affection	*I love to be touched. I love public displays of affection from my partner: holding hands, putting his arm around me, kissing me, and gazing into my eyes. I enjoy it when we casually reach out and touch each other affectionately throughout the day.*
Career Support	*I often work late into the evenings and most weekends in my holistic healing practice, as well as writing and publishing my books. I require my partner to honor, respect, and support me in my many ventures. When I'm frustrated, he will listen to me. When I'm tired, he will hold me. When I'm hungry, he will feed me. When I'm upset, he will kiss me. When I'm overwhelmed, he will tell me how amazing I am.*

LIVING YOUR EXTRAORDINARY LIFE
Guide to Romantic Intimate Relationship

PERSONAL MANUAL *(cont'd)*

Projects and Honey-Dos	*I need an organized, clutter-free home environment. I prefer to hire a housekeeper to clean my house on a weekly basis. I want my partner to share daily chores— like dishes, laundry, yard work, etc.—and pick up after himself. I enjoy it when my partner does the grocery shopping and leaves the cooking to me. I love when my partner willingly helps with my projects, and supports me in doing it my way, without saying, "I told you so," if it doesn't quite turn out. I like having a visible Honey- Do list with plans and deadlines. I like scheduling time each week together to acknowledge and celebrate what's been accomplished and plan what's next.*
Finances	*I need a partner who is financially self-sufficient; values being responsible, wise, and generous with money; and avoids excessive debt. I contribute my own financial stability to the relationship. We willingly seek professional assistance in planning for our future and take the advice and actions provided.*
Accident, Serious Injury, or Illness	*In the event I am unable to care for myself, I want my partner to get assistance from an outside source for my physical care. If I am ever incapacitated, please honor my living will.*
Core Values	*I require a partner who values love, inspiration, empowerment, encouragement, respect, trust, integrity, and friendship. I need a partner who willingly expresses love for me through affection; is inspired by life's possibilities and open to my wisdom and support; enthusiastically encourages and values others; is implicitly trusting and trustworthy; and exhibits a high level of personal integrity. Above all, I want someone who is my best friend.*

LIVING YOUR EXTRAORDINARY LIFE
Guide to Sexual Satisfaction

PERSONAL MANUAL

Initiating Sex	*I want a partner who is responsive when I initiate sex, and I love the feeling of being desired when my partner takes the lead. I have been known to spontaneously join my partner in the shower for frolic and foreplay.*
Foreplay	*I sometimes create the mood by wearing sexy lingerie and inviting my partner to take it off, or dancing naked like a goddess with colorful, silky scarves. I enjoy intensifying the mood by playing my favorite love songs and massaging my lover's body with long, slow strokes.*
	I love it when my partner flirts, teases, and tenderly kisses me softly on my lips, neck, shoulders, and beyond. The thing that puts me immediately in the mood is when my lover gently caresses my face and whispers how beautiful and special I am to him. I am also instantly turned on when my lover appears in the doorway naked, excited to see me.
Lights On/Lights Off Eyes Open/Eyes Closed	*I prefer low light in the room so I can enjoy the visual splendor of making love.*
	I prefer that my partner and I make love with our eyes open. When we're looking into each other's eyes, I am present to the sacredness of our divine connection.
Oral Sex	*Love to get it. Especially love to give it.*
Intercourse	*I especially like it after receiving oral sex. I enjoy trying new positions, and prefer making love face to face. I must have a lover who prioritizes satisfying my needs before his own.*
Following Sex	*I enjoy cuddling in my lover's arms as we drift off together.*
Following Day	*I like being told what a fabulous lover I am and how satisfying the experience was.*

LIVING YOUR EXTRAORDINARY LIFE
Guide to Sexual Satisfaction

PERSONAL MANUAL *(cont'd)*

Preferences	*I like making love in the coziness of my bed—and when the mood strikes—I enjoy having sex in unusual places like on the patio, on the kitchen table, or anywhere out in nature...especially on the beach.*
	I enjoy sex three times a week. My favorite time of day is in the morning when I have lots of energy. I really enjoy Sunday mornings.
	I love when my intimate experiences last for hours. I also like 'nooners' and 'quickies'. There is nothing better than shutting out the world and playing "King for a Day," or "Queen for a Day."
Boundaries	*No multiple partners. No verbal or physical violent behavior. No bondage or S&M.*

When Bernie and I were both satisfied with our answers, and ready to authentically share our manuals, we planned to slip away to a peaceful mountain retreat to have an intimate, uninterrupted conversation where anything could be said and anything could be heard. Unfortunately, circumstances arose that thwarted our plans and we opted to share in the privacy of our living room. We discovered the location had little to do with the profoundness of the experience. So, as long as a location is private and uninterrupted, it's perfect.

The following is an overview of how we shared our desires, expectations, and acknowledgments with nothing missing and nothing left unsaid.

My experience of having these tender conversations with my beloved Bernie about our Guides to Daily Living, Romantic Intimate Relationship, and Sexual Satisfaction was magical.

Before we started sharing, we turned off our phones to minimize distractions and interruptions. I then arranged two chairs so that we could communicate face-to-face, with deliberate eye contact. Next, we agreed to intentionally listen to each other with curiosity, wonderment, and how best we could enrich the quality of our relationship.

Knowing that each person may require a different level of trust and safety to be comfortable revealing intimate details, and that there was no right way to do this, I asked Bernie how he would like to share. He wanted to read and discuss his entire Guide for Daily Living, so that is what we did.

While Bernie was sharing, I focused my full attention on really listening to him, and when he was done, I said, *"It sounds like you are saying...X, Y, Z. Is that what you're saying? Is there anything else you need to add?"*

After each section, we discussed how he could have more of what he wanted—most of which was more quality time with me—and how I could provide that. I took brief notes to capture his needs, wants, and concerns so that we could review them and establish ways to fulfill his desires. We completed by scheduling time to share my Guide for Daily Living later that evening.

My heart felt so expansive after our conversation that all day I was eagerly looking forward to sharing my manual. When I got home from work, we set the intention again before I shared my Guide for Daily Living.

Bernie already knew most of the things I shared about my daily living needs, wants, and concerns. However, there were a few things we made a commitment to improve upon—such as, before Bernie or I start sharing about something that's important to us, we get the other's full attention in order to feel heard.

Since there was nothing wrong, and we weren't trying to work anything out, my experience of sharing our Daily Living Guides was wonderful. We were there because we wanted to share from our hearts what mattered most to us. What naturally arose were ideas and suggestions about how I could make sure that he got what he needed from me, and he knew exactly how to please me—without me expecting him to read my mind.

The following morning we could hardly wait to share both our Guides to Romantic Intimate Relationship and to Sexual Satisfaction. Before we began sharing each Guide, we set the intention again to create a sacred space where anything could be said and anything could be heard.

This time we chose to share section by section—first Bernie shared his, then I shared mine—so we could really listen and discuss our deepest desires and how we could fulfill the other's needs, topic by topic.

When we were done sharing and discussing what we had written, we both experienced the power of love—being present and getting gotten. However, I felt there was still something missing—it was appreciation and acknowledgment.

Starting with my Guide to Daily Living, I went section by section through each Guide, acknowledging Bernie for all the ways I appreciate what he is already providing in each area. Bernie then chose to profoundly acknowledge and appreciate me in one fell swoop for the many ways I continually meet his needs with a generous, accepting, open, and forgiving heart. I was on cloud nine!

When we finished sharing, I was compelled to read to Bernie the letter inviting him to participate in this process—it moved us both to tears. We gazed continuously into each other's eyes for several minutes—bonding at the level of soul—solidifying our love and devotion for one another. The experience was extraordinary and absolute.

With an enduring commitment to create a fabulous future together, we established a weekly meeting to revisit what we discussed so we could evaluate our progress toward enhancing our intimacy. We also agreed to add anything that we noticed was missing and improve upon anything that was not working.

Our weekly meetings have already produced a way to resolve breakdowns and triggers by using code words. For example, when I'm frustrated or overwhelmed with a project, I react with a loud, *"Wa-a-a-ah,"* to which Bernie responds, *"How can I support you, Honey?"* This allows me to release my upset without Bernie trying to fix me or the situation. Another example is when my feelings are hurt, I can express it to Bernie by saying, *"Ouch!"* This allows Bernie to be present to my feelings and implement what would love do right now.

Guidelines for Sharing

There are many ways to share your Guides. Create what works best for you and your partner. Choose who goes first, whether to share section by section, or all at once. The key is to intentionally listen, compassionately discuss any wants, needs, or concerns, and graciously bestow appreciation and acknowledgment for what each of you are already providing. The conversation may also examine whether you're willing to remedy a concern— or not; whether you're willing to accommodate a specific desire—or not; or whether you're willing to align with a particular course of action—or not.

Consider taking each Guide separately, have three conversations on three different days, giving each of you time to integrate what's been communicated, and express appreciation as well as acknowledgment along the way.

Don't let how you should share stop you. Be creative. Get ideas from each other. If one has a preference that works for them, do it their way first. Once you get in the flow, you can evaluate if it's working. If not, choose again.

Regardless of how you chose to share, the most important thing to remember is listening to one another with the intention to understand, which will lead to a completely different outcome than listening only because you are waiting for your turn to speak.

As you continue to integrate everything you're learning about yourself and your partner, notice how your relationship improves and becomes more intimate. By expressing ongoing gratitude for the experience of being loved and loving fully, the law of attraction will provide even more!

Now it's your turn. Follow your heart. Bring all of yourself to this process. It will be worth the risk. Use the ***Living Your Extraordinary Life: Guide to Daily Living, Guide to Romantic, Intimate Relationship,*** and ***Guide to Sexual Satisfaction*** worksheets available for download on my website at www.ExtraordinaryOutcomesPublishing.com/forms.

Sharing may bring you closer, or it could reveal that you and your partner are actually mismatched. If one or both of you have no desire to change or compromise on a particular topic, you can continue to live in a somewhat less than fulfilling relationship, or if the issue is a real deal-breaker, set each other free to love and be loved by someone more compatible. Moving on may not be easy—however, over time you'll begin to feel free to love again.

Keep the channels of communication open with your partner. It's never too late to have a relationship expressing the intimacy you yearn for, and have your needs, desires, and expectations completely fulfilled—with nothing left out.

Conclusion

You can have an extraordinary life! As you apply the concepts in this book, and ask yourself, *"What would love do right now?"* notice how your life becomes richer and more fulfilling in every way. By continuing to resolve and heal the hurtful incidents from your past and choose actions that express love for yourself, the experience of being love at any moment—in any circumstance—is available. This access to being love makes it easier to bring the presence of love to your relationships and your life, rather than waiting, striving, or longing for it to mysteriously appear.

Remember to celebrate and acknowledge the courage it took to examine and release the emotional pain you were holding onto from the past. Now that it is in the past—where it belongs—there is room to create something new. Soon you will be living your life by design—one where you can hardly wait to get up, and one that is overflowing with love, joy, passion, and fulfillment.

I encourage you to review and update your ideals on a regular basis to ensure that nothing is missing, and share the desires and expectations contained in your personal manuals with the people in your life.

Look for the subtle as well as dramatic ways in which your life is improving—how you quiet your mind to hear your heart; how you accept more and complain less; how you respond in new ways to old situations; how you attract new opportunities; how you easily manifest what you say you want—you will see it everywhere! Notice how self-confident, heart-centered, self-expressed, energized, and satisfied you feel.

Along your journey, may what you've created, from the wisdom and knowledge contained in this book, be the beacon of light that illuminates your way forward to living an extraordinary life!

Resources

Amends and Forgiveness

Marmer, Steven. *Forgiveness*
www.prageru.com/courses/life-studies/forgiveness

Ruiz, Don Miguel. *The Four Agreements*
www.miguelruiz.com

Smith, Bob and Wilson, Bill. *The Big Book of Alcoholics Anonymous*
www.aa.org/

Virtue, Doreen. *Healing with the Angels Oracle Cards*
www.angeltherapy.com

Finances

Shin, Laura: Contributor Forbes Personal Finance. *10 Questions to Ask When Choosing a Financial Advisor*
www.forbes.com/sites/laurashin/2013/05/09/10-questions-to-ask-when-choosing-a-financial-advisor/#353ffb403642

Sinetar, Marsha. *Do What You Love and the Money Will Follow*
www.marshasinetar.com

Health

Hay, Louise L. *You Can Heal Your Life*
www.louisehay.com

Institute of Harmonic Science, Phoenix, AZ. *The Higher Vibrations, A Healing Choir*
www.meetup.com/HigherVibrations

Love

Chapman, Gary. *The 5 Love Languages: The Secret to Love That Lasts*
www.5lovelanguages.com/gary-chapman

Jong, Erica. *How to Save Your Own Life*
www.ericajong.com/lovecomesfirst.htm

Purpose and Ideals

Canfield, Jack. *The Success Principles: How to Get From Where You Are to Where You Want to Be*
www.jackcanfield.com/about-jack-canfield

Gawain, Shakti. *Creative Visualization*
www.shaktigawain.com

Landmark Worldwide, LLC. *The Landmark Forum*®
www.landmarkworldwide.com

Raised Vibration. *Vision Boards*
www.raisedvibration.com

Relationships

Armstrong, Allison. *The Queen's Code*®
www.understandmen.com

Davidson, Michael. *Simple Wisdom for Complex Lives*
www.tinybuddha.com

Hellinger, Bert. *Family Constellation According to Hellinger*
www2.hellinger.com/home

Self-Expression

Cameron, Julia. *The Artist's Way*
juliacameronlive.com

Spruce, Georganne. *Awakening to the Dance: A Journey to Wholeness*
www.georgannespruce.com/the-book

Triggers

Goodson, Zachary. *How to Deal with Painful Emotional Triggers in Your Relationships*
www.tinybuddha.com/blog/how-to-deal-with-painful-emotional-triggers-in-your-relationships

Victoria Benoit, M.C. *Center for Extraordinary Outcomes*

We provide holistic healing through a variety of modalities. To learn more, please visit my website ExtraordinaryOutcomes.com and explore the sites below:

Bartlett D.C. N.D., Richard. *Matrix Energetics®*
www.matrixenergetics.com

Callahan Ph.D., Roger. *Thought Field Therapy®*
www.rogercallahan.com/callahan.php

Dosick Rabbi Ph.D. D.D., Wayne. *Spiritual Healing for Indigos*
www.soulbysoul.com

Kaufman-Dosick M.S.W., Ellen. *Soul Memory Discovery*
www.soulmemorydiscovery.com

Lindstead NHD CNC, Stephen. *Scalar Heart Connection®*
www.scalarheartconnection.com

Wordsworth M.A., Chloe Faith. *Resonance Repatterning®*
www.resonancerepatterning.net

Yuen D.C., Kam. *Yuen Method*
www.yuenmethod.com

Acknowledgments

This book was made possible with the unwavering support of the following wonderful people who helped during the many phases of its birth. I begin by acknowledging myself for listening to my nudge to write and for my dedication and perseverance along the way; then, Tom Bird, the book whisperer, and his wonderful staff with the Publish Now program who never gave up on me; and a special recognition to William Murphy, my book buddy, whose support calls made all the difference. Finally, all of my dear friends—especially, Tarra of Sedona, Dr. Roxane Beck, Angela Johnson, Mimi Planas, Rudrani Brand, and Linda Green, as well as Dian Daniel, and the members of Raised Vibration—who have been at my side every step of the way.

I have acquired and integrated a plethora of knowledge from the following remarkable experts who directly influenced me and the ideas in this book. I am extremely grateful to my professors at the University of Phoenix®; leaders at Landmark Worldwide, LLC; Chloe Faith Wordsworth, M.A., developer of Resonance Repatterning®; Dr. Stephen Lindstead, developer of Scalar Heart Connection®; Ellen Kaufman-Dosick, M.S.W., developer of Soul Memory Discovery; Dr. Wayne Dosick, developer of Spiritual Healing for Indigos; Dr. Roger Callahan, developer of Thought Field Therapy®; Dr. Kam Yuen, developer of the Yuen Method; Dr. Richard Bartlett, developer of Matrix Energetics®; Allison Armstrong, developer of The Queen's Code® workshop series; and all my mentors and coaches over the years.

With the deepest gratitude humanly possible, thank you to Paula Hofmeister, my extraordinary editor, a wordsmith whose unending attention to style and detail is off the charts; and to Betsy McGrew, my award-winning graphic designer, for her intuitive vision and relentless dedication to designing and formatting this book, along with its beautiful cover, and my fabulous www.ExtraordinaryOutcomesPublishing.com website.

I am who and where I am today due to the love of my mother, father, and siblings—all silent supporters of my novel adventures, although often beyond their realm of conventional thinking, they support me just the same.

Last but not least, I extend profound appreciation to my biggest fan, my Beloved Bernie, whose unconditional love for me and outstanding support for my greatness has been a solid foundation from which I continue to discover and explore—the writer within.

About the Author

I'm Victoria Benoit, Author and Publisher, residing in Phoenix, Arizona with my beloved partner, Bernie. I am a fun-loving, optimistic woman living an extraordinarily rich life, filled with passion, love, and adventure. Along with writing, I enjoy ballroom and country dancing, singing, biking, hiking, golf, spending time in nature, and traveling to beaches around the world. My friends and family are especially dear to me no matter what we're doing.

I grew up in Milwaukee, WI, with my brother and two sisters. At 20 years old, I seized an opportunity to move to the big city of Chicago, knowing no one, relying solely on my own sense of adventure. The next 18 years were both routine and eventful. While having a successful career in medical ultrasound and being married and divorced—twice—I began my spiritual journey of personal growth through the study of metaphysics.

In 1989, I decided it was time to move on—from the Windy City to Phoenix, the Valley of the Sun. Shortly after moving, I was forced to change careers due to a physical injury. In examining what to do next, I saw that through my work as a neonatal ultrasound technologist, I had experienced my natural ability to provide a space of profound love and compassion for couples in the initial stage of grief over the loss of their baby. I applied this insight to create a new career in supporting people through tough times.

The next step in my journey was to obtain my Master's Degree and begin working as a Licensed Professional Counselor. I was quickly frustrated with my clients' lack of progress using traditional methodologies. I decided to study other approaches to support people in creating lives they loved. This guided me to become a Certified Resonance Repatterning® practitioner and teacher. I then began working with private clients, part time, using this process to identify and clear their unconscious patterns. Session after session they reported experiencing extraordinary outcomes in their lives.

Based on my results with private clients, I left traditional counseling completely in 1996, and opened the Center for Extraordinary Outcomes, ExtraordinaryOutcomes.com. Along with seeing clients, I started teaching Resonance Repatterning internationally; I developed workshops; and continued to study and implement additional holistic healing therapies in my practice. Over the years, it became apparent that I needed to stop teaching and start writing to fulfill my desire to impact even more people.

I absolutely love the difference I make in the world! I am committed to helping people live a life they love—one that is overflowing with love, joy, passion, and fulfillment.

Stay Connected

Thank you for purchasing this book. I trust you enjoyed it.
To inspire others, please write a review and share an
extraordinary outcome that made a difference in your life
on Amazon.com, Goodreads.com, and/or
ExtraordinaryOutcomesPublishing.com.

Be the first to hear about my new releases and bargains.
Sign up at the link provided below to be on the VIP list.
I promise not to share your email with anyone or clutter your inbox.
www.ExtraordinaryOutcomesPublishing.com/stay-connected/

www.ingramcontent.com/pod-product-compliance
Lightning Source LLC
Chambersburg PA
CBHW072145020426
42334CB00018B/1887